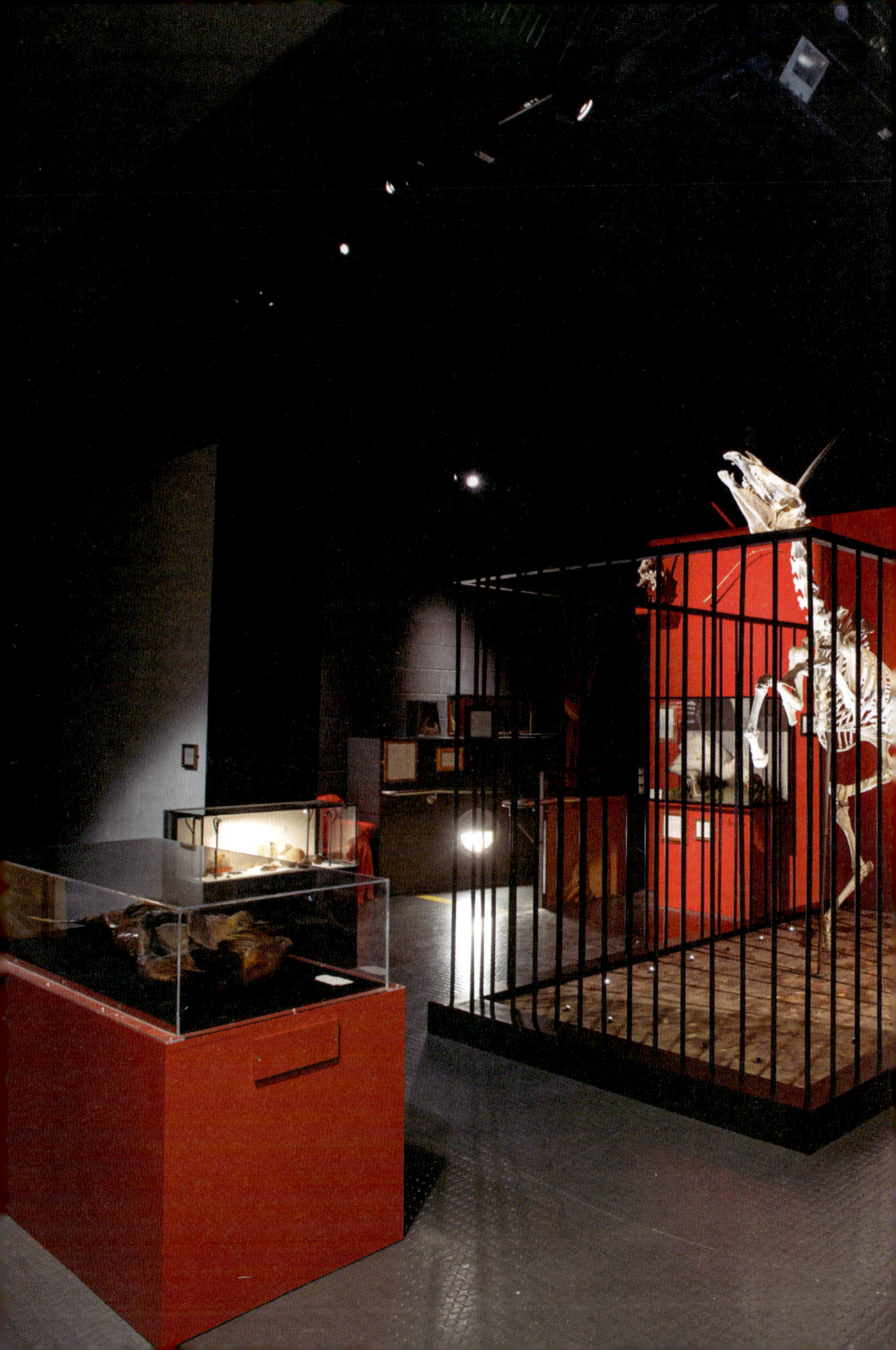

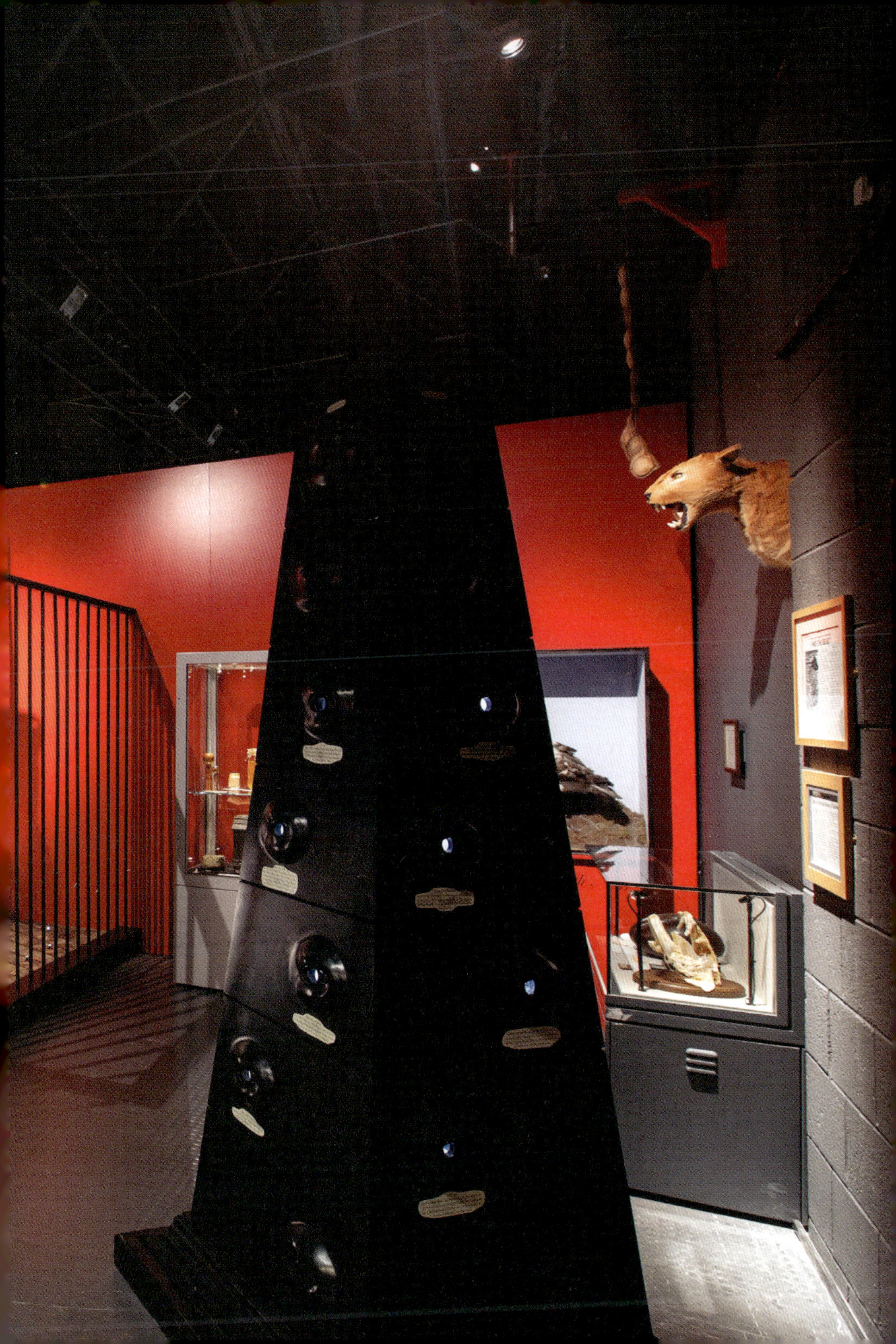

The Hosting of the Sidhe

The Host is riding from Knocknarea
And over the grave of Clooth-na-bare;
Caolte tossing his burning hair
And Niamh calling Away, come away:
Empty your heart of its mortal dream.
The winds awaken, the leaves whirl round,
Our cheeks are pale, our hair is unbound,
Our breasts are heaving, our eyes are a-gleam,
Our arms are waving, our lips are apart;
And if any gaze on our rushing band,
We come between him and the deed of his hand,
We come between him and the hope of his heart.
The host is rushing 'twixt night and day,
And where is there hope or deed as fair?
Caolte tossing his burning hair,
And Niamh calling Away, come away.

W.B.Yeats

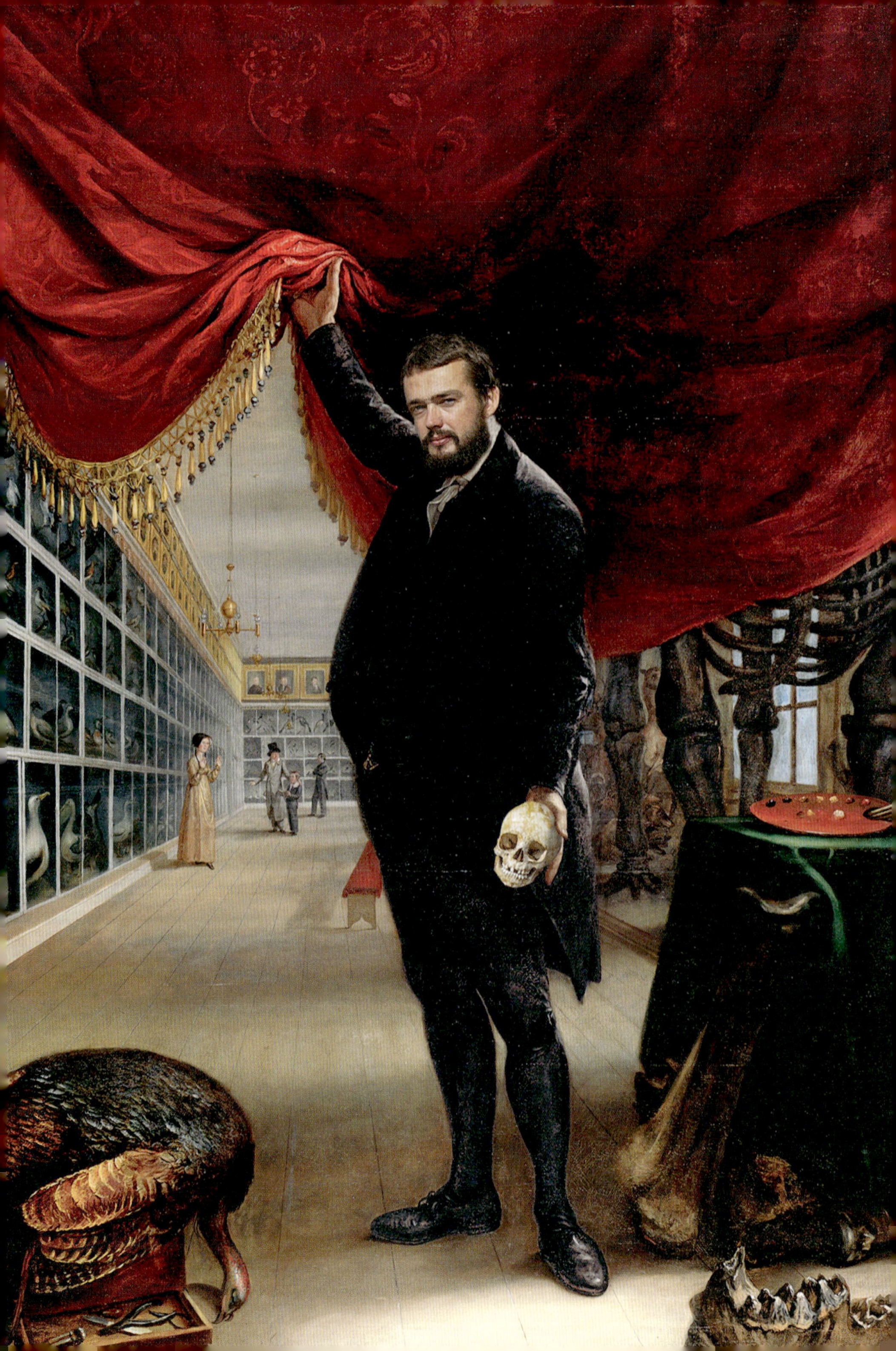

THE INFECTED MUSEUM

VIKTOR WYND'S UNNATURAL HISTORY MUSEUM

WITHIN

THE NATIONAL MARITIME MUSEUM, CORNWALL.

MARCH 2020 – DECEMBER 2022

WITH CONTRIBUTIONS FROM

ADRIAN DANNATT, MARK DION, RICHARD DOUGHTY, ARTHUR MACGREGOR & RICHARD PELL

PHOTOS BY KIRSTIN PRISK

CONTENTS

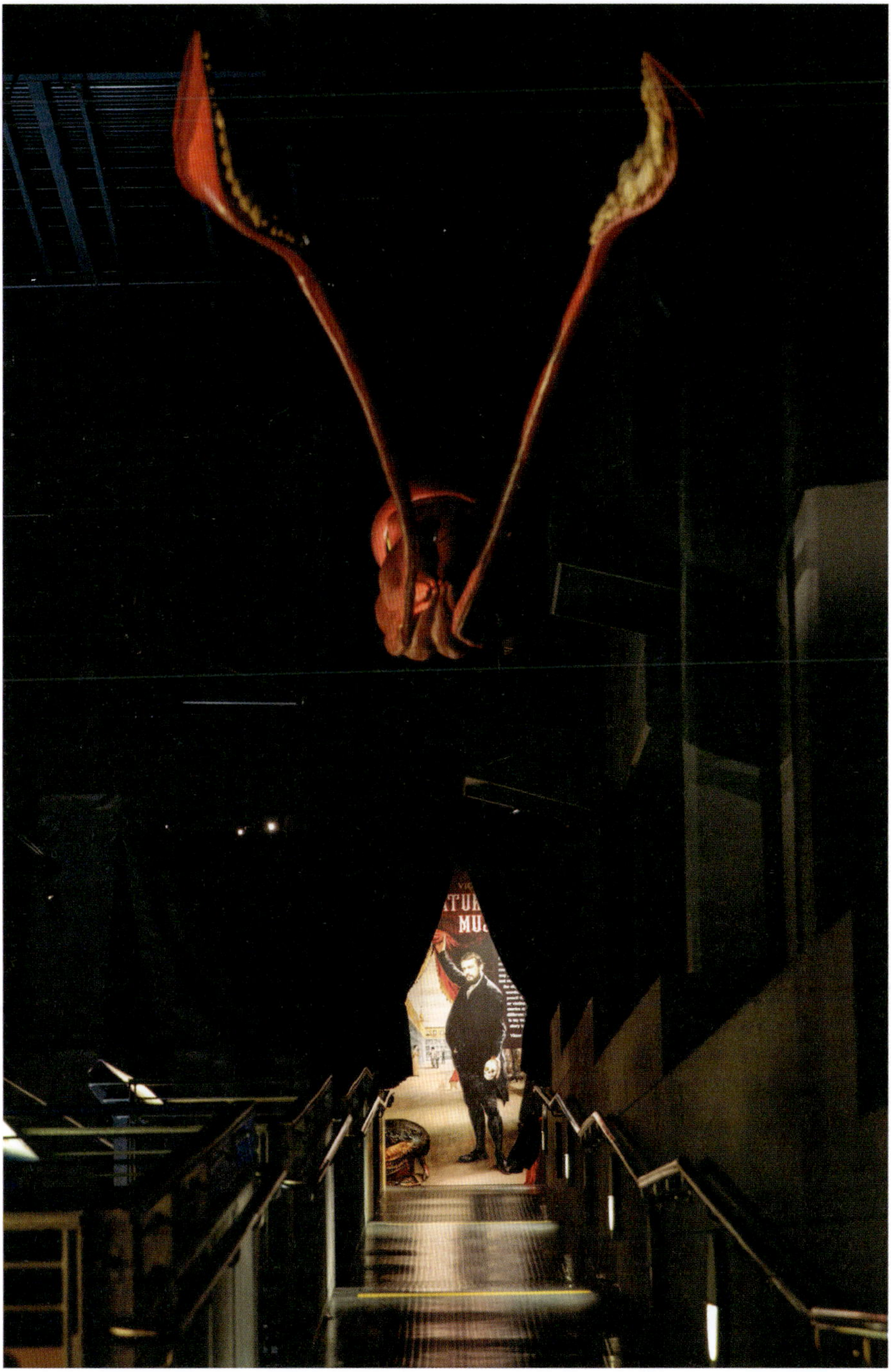

FOREWORD

Richard Doughty, Museum Director

Working with Viktor Wynd is rather like experiencing an antiquarian cabinet of curiosity for the first time. Both the man and the extraordinary objects he has assembled, generate a palpable sense of awe and delight.

The bewitching world he presents to his viewers is as wonderful as it is bizarre but then Wynd is no ordinary museum curator, he is a magician, adroit at breathing fresh life into his exhibits, often with a flamboyant flourish but invariably with an imperceptible sleight of hand.

I rejoice in Wynd's playfulness, for it is this which gives him licence to be open to the infinite possibility of meanings he ascribes to objects he has collected. However, his sense of mischief, devilment and humour (rarely evidenced in museum spaces) bely the true nature of his passions – a desire to disrupt, disturb and ultimately transgress our 'normal' connections to the physical world around us.

As an artist and collector, this is what Wynd has brought to the National Maritime Museum Cornwall with the reincarnation of his UnNatural History Museum. His captivating installation, quite unlike anything else in our Museum, nonetheless picks up and plays with many of the ideas, themes and displays found in its wider galleries, particularly our major exhibition 'Monsters of the Deep: Science Fact and Fiction'.

Wynd presents the viewer with objects, some seemingly mundane, some astonishing, some shocking, that cause us to question what we think of as natural or unnatural, real or fake, beautiful or grotesque (though, with Wynd it is never as simple or binary as this).

Encountering stories and 'hand-written' labels that are at once wilfully idiosyncratic, blatantly untrue and true (for a certain value of 'true') our casual acceptance of evidence and authority in a museum space is unsettled.

At the risk of sounding pompous (something I suspect Wynd would find both amusing and irresistible), I would argue Museums, as cultural organisations, are better, more relevant and more interesting when we constantly question the objects we collect, the meanings we ascribe to them, the stories we recount, the voices who tell them and the audiences they reach.

...and besides where else would our visitors get an opportunity to gaze upon an actual unicorn skeleton...I mean what more could you ask for?

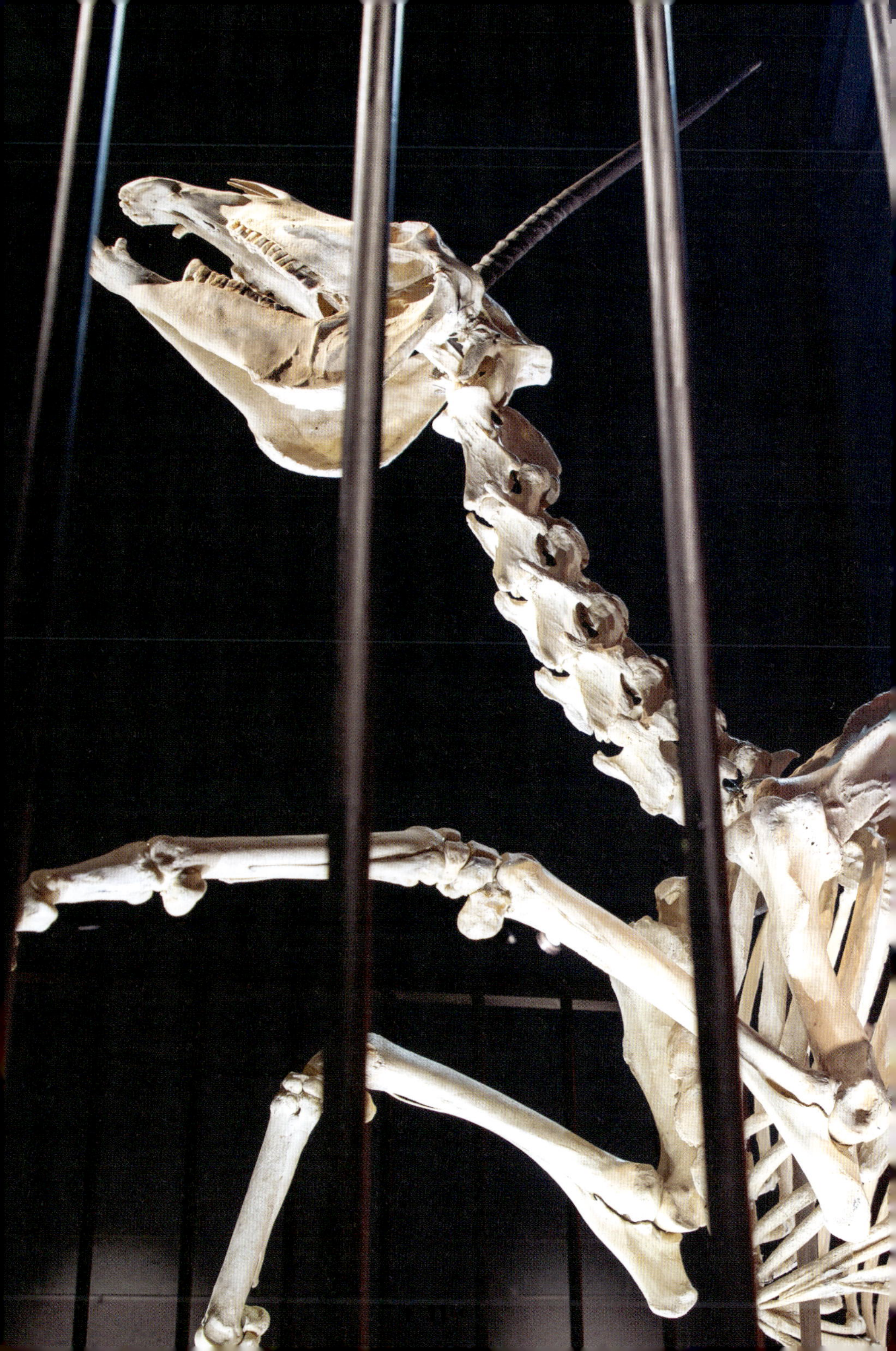

THE MOST INTERESTING MAN IN ENGLAND

Adrian Dannatt

Really, in the end, or rather right here at the beginning, it would be accurate to call Viktor Wynd the most interesting man in England; for here is someone entirely imaginary, strictly fictional, yet enormously physically real, a huge, towering giant bearded embodiment of Anglo-Saxon meaty being, who has single-handedly magicked into existence the most unusual museum in all of Christendom, a fatal lure for every crusading lover of olde curiosite, disciple of oddity.

Oh today so little true mystery remains, blame our giant blinking banks of search-engines mining data day and night, our little hand-held algorithms that instantly answer every imaginable question- yet Wynd has somehow managed to remain a genuine enigma. It may be certain that this is not his only name and who dares know his true nomenclature nor age, where he comes from, who he is, or why, the origin of this species, education, breeding, lineage, escutcheon even, "the Somerset Wynds?" No, all is zero, dark as a Limehouse night.

But what we do know is that the Viktor Wynd Museum of Curiosities, Fine Art & UnNatural History, established in 2014 and based in the cruel heart of Hackney, epicentre of the East End, is the most improbable and enjoyable of experiences, a tiny portal in a still relatively insalubrious row of shops, allowing one to enter this veritable kingdom of marvels. It is crammed to the rafters with madness and daring, dark and full and fascinating, impossible and indispensable as a dispensary. To quote its founding declaration, 'this museum will merely display everything that has glittered & caught the eye of it's founder – from rare priceless marvels of the natural and scientific worlds like Dodo Bones or speculum to the intriguing beauty of McDonald's Happy Meal Toys, from old master etchings to prison inmates & mad women's doodles, occultists paintings and pop art prints, the horrors and wonders of nature, two headed kittens and living coral.'

Evidently there is nowhere else like this, not on the ocean lashed final salty pier of Coney Island nor bunkers of Tasmania, a place to get regally smashed on illegal absinthe, for they serve it here in secret

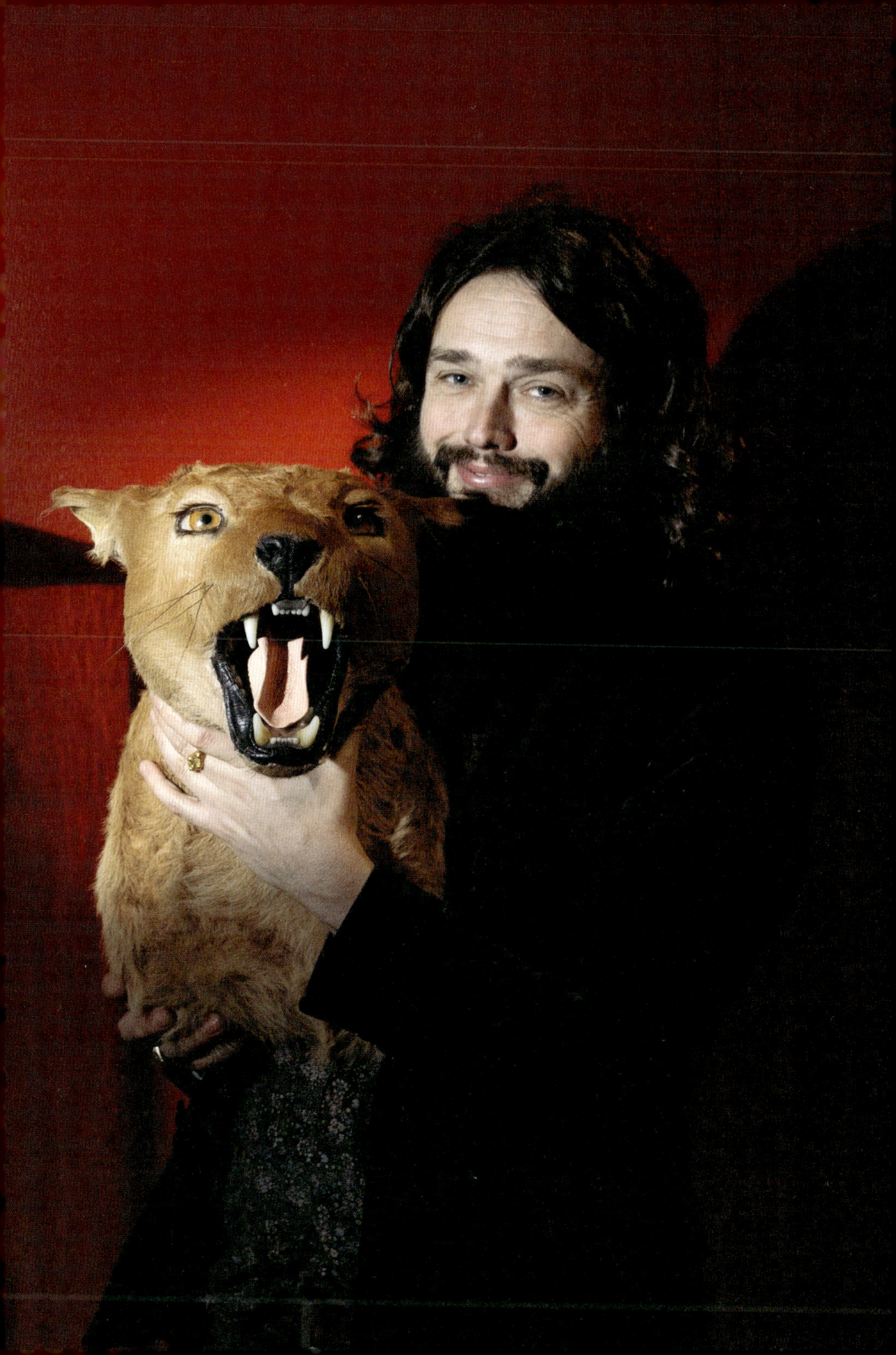

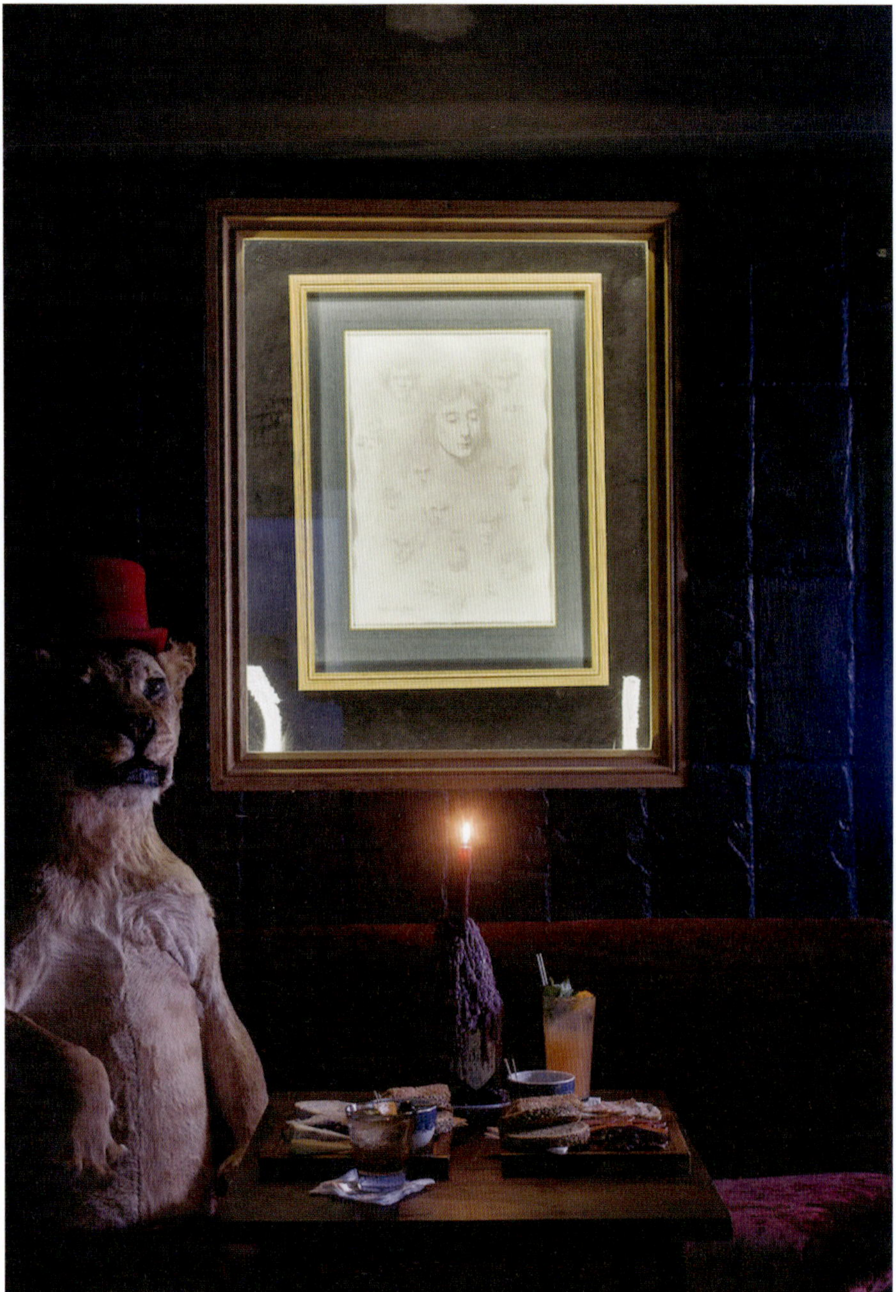

The (Austin Osman) Spare Room

from their ancient bar, whilst admiring the sheer perversity of the owner's artefacts, the sheer range of peculiarity Wynd has hoarded to himself over the difficult decades. Herewithin the gloaming can be found some and all of the following; taxidermied goat, radioactive seashells, a horse's stomach infected by botflies, extinct birds, a potentially human sarcophagus, a gold-plated hippopotamus skull once belonging to cocaine czar Escobar, a cyclops brain, jars with the 'preserved front bottoms of Victorian prostitutes', a lock of King Elvis's hair and actual works of art by such randomly esteemed figures as Mervyn Peake, Stephen Tennant, Jeff Koons and Tracey Emin.

Rightly enough it is hardly surprising that thousands of spellbound fans have made this journey into the heart of Hackney to get drunk and revel in the Wyndian inner-world, not to mention regular visits from every sort of willing celebrity whether writers such as Günter Grass and Jose Saramago, filmmaker Alejandro Jodorowsky or even Stephen Hawking lui-même; and equally impressive one might mention le tout gratin of rock'n'roll aristocracy from Prince to Bowie who all flocked here as if hypnotised by a fellow miracle; for to quote the aforementioned Thin White Duke, who used to call Mr Wynd on a regular basis for late night confabulation, 'every time I feel fascination I just can't stand still, I've got to use her, fascination moves sweeping near me, fascination takes a part of me.'

This all, and more, so much more, is captured and elucidated in a beautiful new exhibition which has come drifting ashore to Falmouth town, so suitable a port-of-call for such swaggering brigandry and salt-tanged strangeness.

For indeed the sea and its myriad denizens, animal, mammal, and everything in -between, are at the very core of Wynd's collections, perhaps even the secret cornerstone of all his lore; after all he owns not only a genuine mermaid (which are rare) but also a bottle of wine from the cellar of Patrick O'Brian, the greatest of 20th century naval writers, as well as a cast cast by his hero Dr Maturin, not to mention sting ray tails and ancient sponges, catfish and radioactive shells, all clogging here the foul mouth of the ocean, that veritable larynx of the seven seas.

But Wynd has, despite or perhaps thanks to being so imaginary an spirit, already done many many things in his manifold lives, more than several of them in defiance of our prissy rules and regulations, our social codes, no more fearing the illegal than the dangerous. Perhaps the easiest way to understand his existence and intention is to see it as a long-running highly ambitious conceptual art project, the self-creation of a personality, 'the Wynd', regardless of the usual rules of chronology and factual identity, some ultimate meta-fiction.

Utterly his own man, somehow Wynd managed to make his way from bosky Oxfordshire to the throbbing slums of Tampa (of which one is always tempted to paraphrase Miller's Quiet Days in Clichy and suggest instead Light Days in Tampa) where he enrolled as a hardworking student at the University of South Florida.

Indeed it was thanks to the highly prestigious fellowship set up by the leading pop artist James Rosenquist that Wynd was thus lured west and soon found himself - in every sense - as a cerebral soi-disant 'conceptual' artist, industriously producing his first cultural objets, not least, like a resplendent North American butterfly from a shy Anglo-Saxon pupae... himself!

Could anyone have suspected back in this Floridian art school that the newly minted Wynd would one day create his own empire of oddity and crown himself the strangest of all denizens of London's deepest east end? Curiously enough, having fled extremely west as a student and lingered in sweaty Tampa until the ripe age of 28 Wynd has subsequently committed himself to heading further and further east, as if sprung from some foreign catapult, and now found himself like some demonic gentleman farmer in furthest Suffolk, ultimate edge of England, busy growing dangerous plants and making frightening figurines worthy of some Arthur Machen latter-day ritual in the potting shed.

Kissed by genius, the Wyndian curriculum vitae includes everything from studying Francophile civilisation at the Sorbonne to slaving away like some latter-day Hakim Bey on the more obscure areas of Islamic heresy, not to mention a series of one-man sell-out shows with such memorable titles as 'Why I Think I'm so Fucking Special - It's All About Me' and 'The Sorrows of Young Wynd.' But tiring of the obligations of self-promotion the maestro maverick turned to larger ambitions than creating mere art things.

Nursing the networked ego of the true entrepreneur Wynd became chancellor of a pataphysical organization entitled 'The Last Tuesday Society' and as such launched some spectacular and highly publicised events; these included a series of masquerade balls attended by over 6,000 people, complete with naked orchestras and golden youth, culminating in an immortal summer ball called Wyndstock which took over every crevice of Houghton Hall, one of Britain's grandest stately homes indeed once the berth of that country's first prime minister Mr Walpole.

Eccentricity is of course the ghastly curse of such figures as Wynd, especially should they happen to hail from England; there are many nobler words to choose to describe so protean and perverse a personality and yet the endlessly renewable cliché of the 'Eccentric Englishman' (an 'EE' worthy of the poet Cummings) seems impossible to overcome or firmly replace. Like Alastair Crowley, who only managed to overcome the selfsame accusations of eccentricity by creating instead the equally alliterative yet far more potent label of 'the wickedest man in the world', doubtless it will take murder or narcotic imbroglio for Wynd's true stature to be rescued from slapdash journalese.

Lovingly curated and lavishly mounted (as we all wish to be mounted) this latest exhibition should also add a massive dollop of gravitas to the man's standing; not least its accompanying notes and authorial museum labels will allow the public to realise that Wynd is really such a good writer, an autobiographical wizard, especially when he deals so elegantly, even amusingly, with that black dog of depression which has long run alongside him, dark double of his manic creativity, whose central place in his life here can be acknowledged with a weary grace. Even in just a throwaway aperçu on one of his most fleeting exhibits, say the crumbs of David Bowie's biscuit, Wynd never fails to mint mischief from the bittersweet melancholia of his disposition, as delightful as dyspeptic.

Last but altogether least this exhibition heralds a sort of 'portable Wynd', a perverse version of Marcel Duchamp's Boîte-en-valise containing all his life's work, which can bravely bob forth on the high seas of the international institutional curatorial circuit for centuries to come. For this exhibition perhaps provides a delicious entrée, a crunchy starter, to whet the appetites of those of us who have the time and sizzle to dare venture into his unique parallel universe. And thus inspired it seems certain that vast swarths of the West Country, hordes of them, will feel it necessary to finally gird their loins and head down to Mare Street, disguised if necessary, wrapped in clandestine rural innocence, to treat themselves to a lethal and illegal cocktail at the final headquarter itself of all such vast Wyndiana.

Adrian Dannatt is an occasional actor, artist, curator and writer, his latest exhibition being 'Impasse Ronsin' at the Museum Tinguely, Basel and his last book 'Doomed and Famous' from Sequence Press, New York.

MUSEUM BUILDING AS AN ART FORM

Mark Dion

Museums are transformative spaces. They can redirect the trajectory of lives, through inspiration and awe. I make this argument as one who has been shaped by my affinity to museums, one who still recalls with some clarity my first visit to a museum on a second grade class field trip to The New Bedford Whaling Museum. What was this place I asked myself? It was not a store, school, or church and unlike those spaces it did not seems to want to convince me of something or sell me anything. I was enamored and wonder struck, but of course quite wrong. Museums do want to sell us something.

Like my friend Viktor Wynd, and a handful of other artists, my life and art has crystallized through a dangerous attraction to museums of all scales, periods and locations. There is something desperate and hungry about this enthrallment, perhaps expressed to best by Susan Sontag, who once confessed to me that she too was "a museum junkie". Museum addicts and professionals experience museums differently from the general public. We tend to sail through museums at fast clip for our first tour, taking the place in as an entirety before circling back for a closer look at exhibition details, architecture, display furniture and labels. We delight in mistakes, out of date design and typography, less then perfect specimens, under appreciated hidden galleries, the patina of use. Museum connoisseurs hunt for untouched spaces, feeling the thrill of time travel as we enter a gallery still installed as it was the day the institution opened. We are often also fortunate to be as familiar with the back of house as the public exhibition spaces. This speaks less to a position of privilege and more to a persistence of will.

Museum enthusiasts know that remarkable museums come in all scales and can be found in surprising locations. Great little museums can have tight focus, like a mouse trap museum or lunch box museum. They may also be shockingly expansive, like a museum of time in a tiny town on the edge of the Colombian jungle. Museums can be the work of a vast staff of experts, or the vision of a single mad collector.

As much as museums may delight and inspire, they also have a lot to answer for as the arbitrators the official story of any society. As the showcases of nationalism, problematic racial politics, and the ideologies of a pernicious sense of progress and the domination of nature, what bourgeois museums promote and conceal is always in the forefront of the discriminating visitor's mind. As dismal as being the mere mouthpiece of the ruling class can be, perhaps the greatest crime of any museum is to be boring.

Viktor Wynd employs museum building as an art form. Some draw and paint, some take photos or sculpt but Wynd makes museums. In fact he makes a museum of museums. In this way he has a deep affinity to the Wunderkammer assemblers of the past, who firmly locate themselves in the center of the cosmology they reenact through their collections. He also has a kinship to the proprietors of eccentric home-made museums found in remote locations across the globe. What Wynd does, however is use the history museum display and the status of the exhibition itself as an arbitrator of truth, as a hilarious training ground for skeptical inquiry. Wynd's marvelous museum spaces are some of the most captivating interrogations into how we know what we know. A Viktor Wynd project challenges viewers, provoking through the dexterous deployment of puzzles, tricks and traps. Like David Wilson's Museum of Jurassic Technology and The Museum of Innocence of Orhan Pamuk, Wynd's museums do something almost unheard of in contemperary museum exhibition design, they assume the viewer to be intelligent.

Mark Dion is an American conceptual artist best known for his use of scientific presentations in his installations.

PARALLEL MUSEOLOGICAL WORLDS

ARTHUR MACGREGOR

Wynd and I inhabit parallel museological worlds. Mine is bounded by the impulse to document, describe, interrogate and contextualize the component parts of collections; I take account of their functions, geographical origins and societal value to their producers, as well as their appeal to those who, in bringing them together and organizing them, transform assemblages of objects into meaningful collections. As a pursuit, it may sound prosaic in the extreme, but the process is one that holds the possibility, at least, of conjuring meaning and significance out of mute objects – or rather, of giving them a voice so that they may express their inherent values for themselves.

By contrast, Wynd's skills lie in articulating specimens so as to invest them with an entirely new spectrum of possibilities that are far from inherent: the construction of imaginative identities and interpretations carries his exhibits beyond the literal world to a realm of his own creation, where they elaborate their own histories like characters in a fictional story, inviting us to leave behind our humdrum world and to join them in theirs. Yet not all his treasures are self-creations: many are stumbled upon or deliberately sought out with the tenacity that characterizes all born collectors. As a result, the act of browsing Viktor's installations or the cabinets in his Museum of Curiosities, Fine Art & UnNatural History is to move imperceptibly from natural to constructed curiosity and seamlessly back again.

The process is a highly visual one, but while other such installations are apt to remain mute – even impenetrable – there is also a strong literary dimension to Wynd's creations: museum labels by their nature tend to evade notice (unless to give rise to complaint at some unforgiveable inaccuracy), but here the dream-like world of the display is enlarged and invested with literary texture. There can never have been labels so insistent, for all their calligraphic quirkiness – 'READ ME!', they seem to demand, and indeed they prove irresistible. Viktor has aptly described himself as 'a writer who presents his novel on handwritten museum labels', but illustrated fiction can scarcely achieve the degree of mutual inter-dependence that characterizes these presentations, made all the more tangible by the prosaic matter-of-factness of the documentary record they present: a mummified fairy 'entrusted

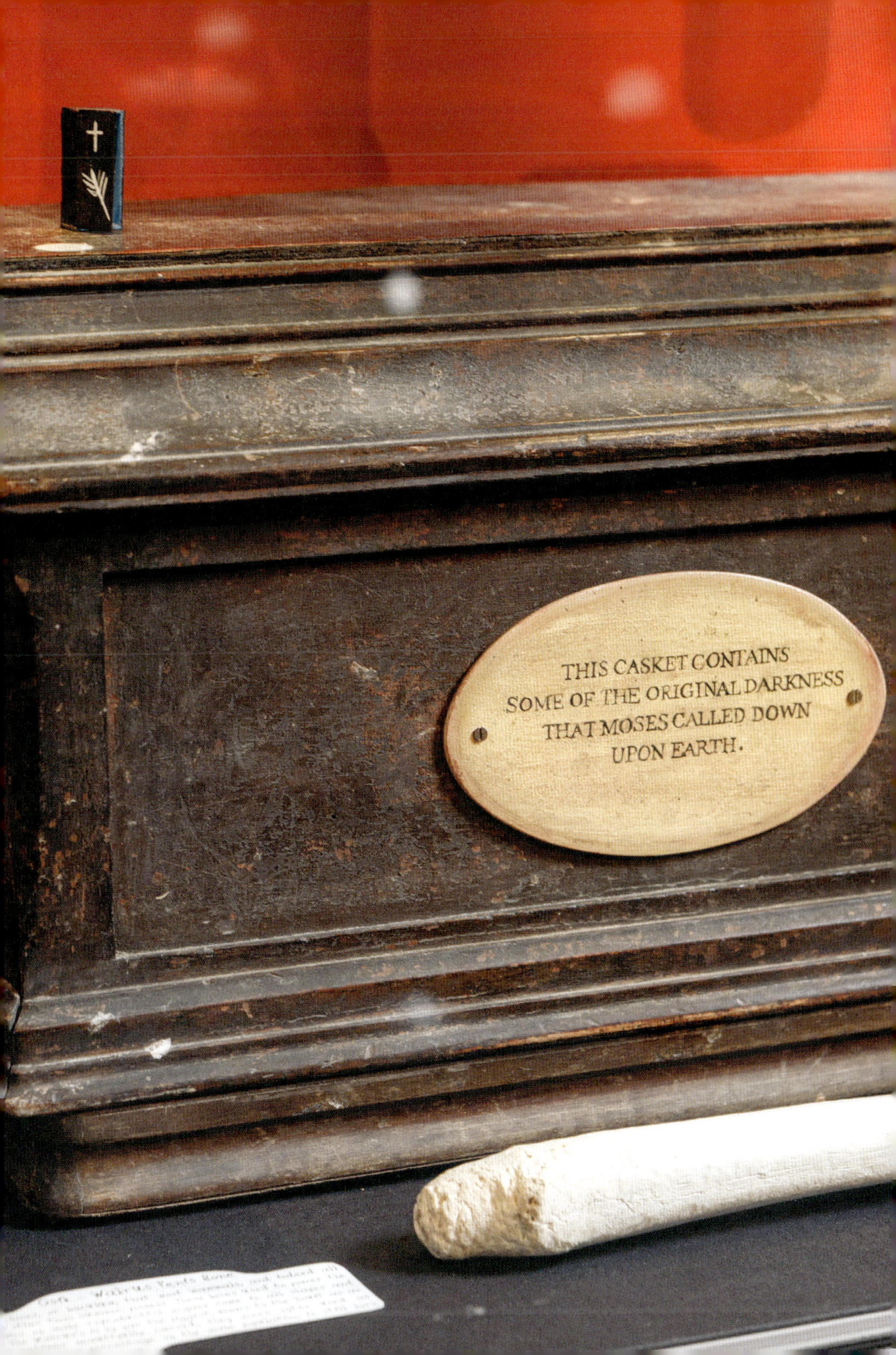
THIS CASKET CONTAINS
SOME OF THE ORIGINAL DARKNESS
THAT MOSES CALLED DOWN
UPON EARTH.

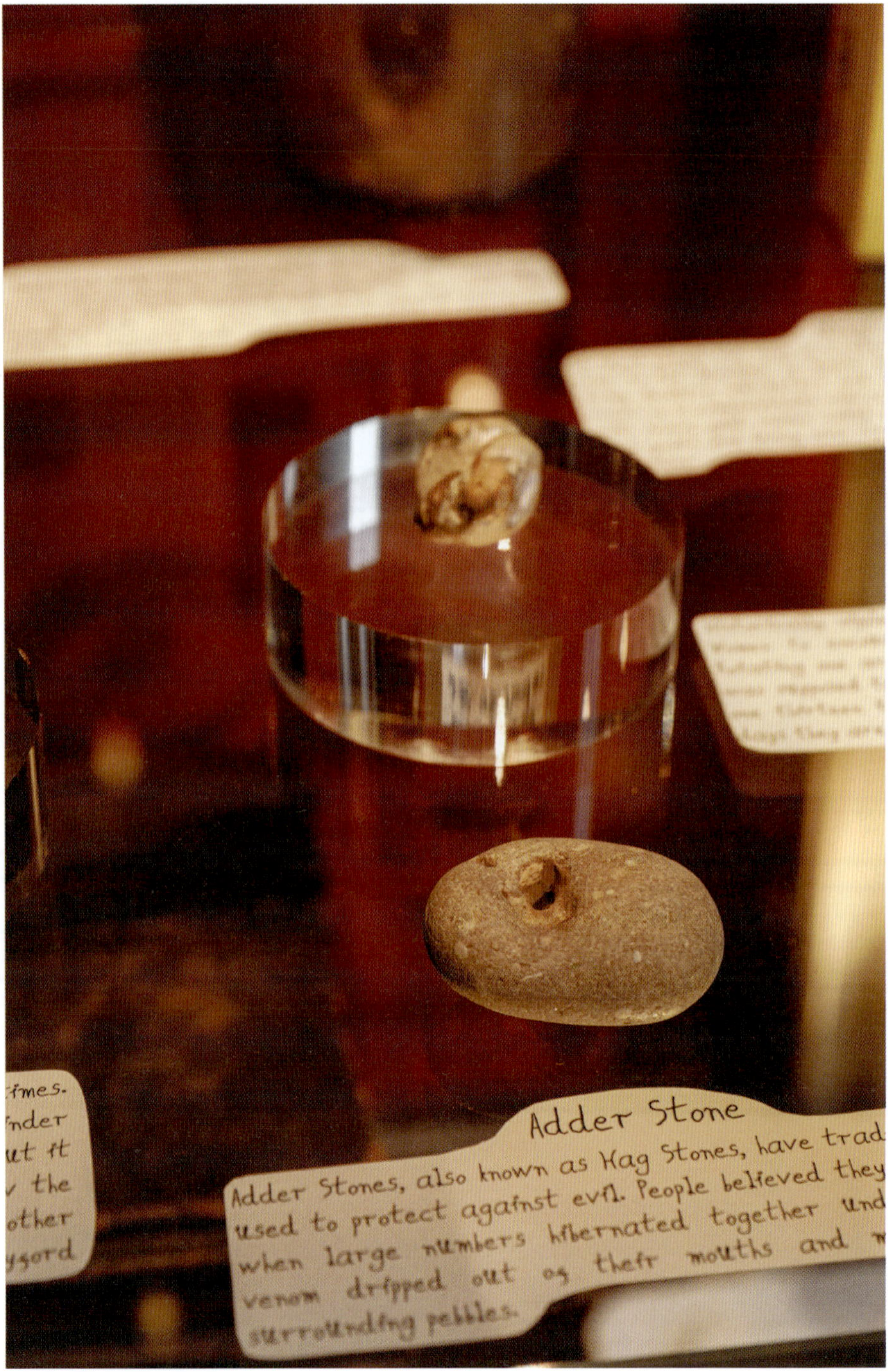
Adder Stone
Adder Stones, also known as Hag Stones, have trad
used to protect against evil. People believed they
when large numbers hibernated together und
venom dripped out of their mouths and
surrounding pebbles.

to me by Alice O'Connor in Aughlean. Co. Mayo ... 12 October 1999' claims our credence with its detailed provenance; a plaster cast of the foot of a selkie, found in flagrante with an intended victim on the island of Hoy on 18 March 1802, first appeared at auction in 1842 – a collection history longer (and scarcely less credible) than that proclaimed by many antiquities offered on the market; a stuffed Labrador duck (Camptorynchus labradorius), extinct since 1878 and now well beyond the scope of living memory, occupies a status scarcely less remote or intangible than that of the mermaids and unicorns on display. In the tradition of the greatest Continental Wunderkammern, the status of the collection is further cemented by tokens of living treasures who have previously looked upon the exhibition: 'Sir David Attenborough's biscuit', not consumed with the cup of tea he was offered on a visit to the Museum of Curiosities on 'III.X.MMXII'.

On reflection, maybe our respective aims have more in common than might at first appear. The ambition to make objects speak can manifest itself in more ways than one, but Wynd's manufactured histories (if that is indeed what they are) add an extra dimension to the objects he curates for us, so that we that we respond to them imaginatively as well as rationally.

Arthur MacGregor is a British academic and author credited with inventing the idea of the history of museums. MacGregor has spent most of his career at the Ashmolean, before his appointment as director of the Society of Antiquaries. He has been president of the Society for the History of Natural History since 2015.

AN INCOMPLETE CATALOG OF ITEMS IN THE EXHIBITION

I. I Believe in Miracles

This Unicorn Skeleton was used my Mr. Wynd to propose. The skeleton was sneaked into his house on Valentine's day 2012 whilst his intended was out and Mr. Wynd placed his Great Grandmother's engagement ring on the end of the horn.

II. Swoose

The Only Known Taxidermied Example of a Swan Goose Hybrid in The World
SWAN & GOOSE HYBRID. HATCHED APRIL 1910. DIED MAY 1924.

Beeston Priory. Sheringham.

"A bird prodigy of evil and hybrid character is the despair of a Norfolk farm. It rejoices in the name of the 'swoose', a portmanteau word indicating its origin, for its father was a swan and its mother a goose!"
The Daily Mail, 1920

"There is at present living, at a farmhouse near Cromer, a hybrid Swan. This anomalous bird, which is the produce of a male Mute Swan and a female domestic Goose, both of them the property of Mrs. A. T. Eeynolds, of Beeston Priory, was hatched in April, 1910. Another was hatched with it, which unfortunately was subsequently killed: there being no gander on the place their parentage is apparently beyond dispute. As will be seen from one of the photographs which Mrs. Eeynolds has had taken of it, this hybrid is more like a Swan than a Goose in shape, and its long neck, which at times it doubles up in Swan fashion, contributes to the similarity. In colouring it rather more resembles the Goose."
The Zoologist Monthly Journal, 1920.

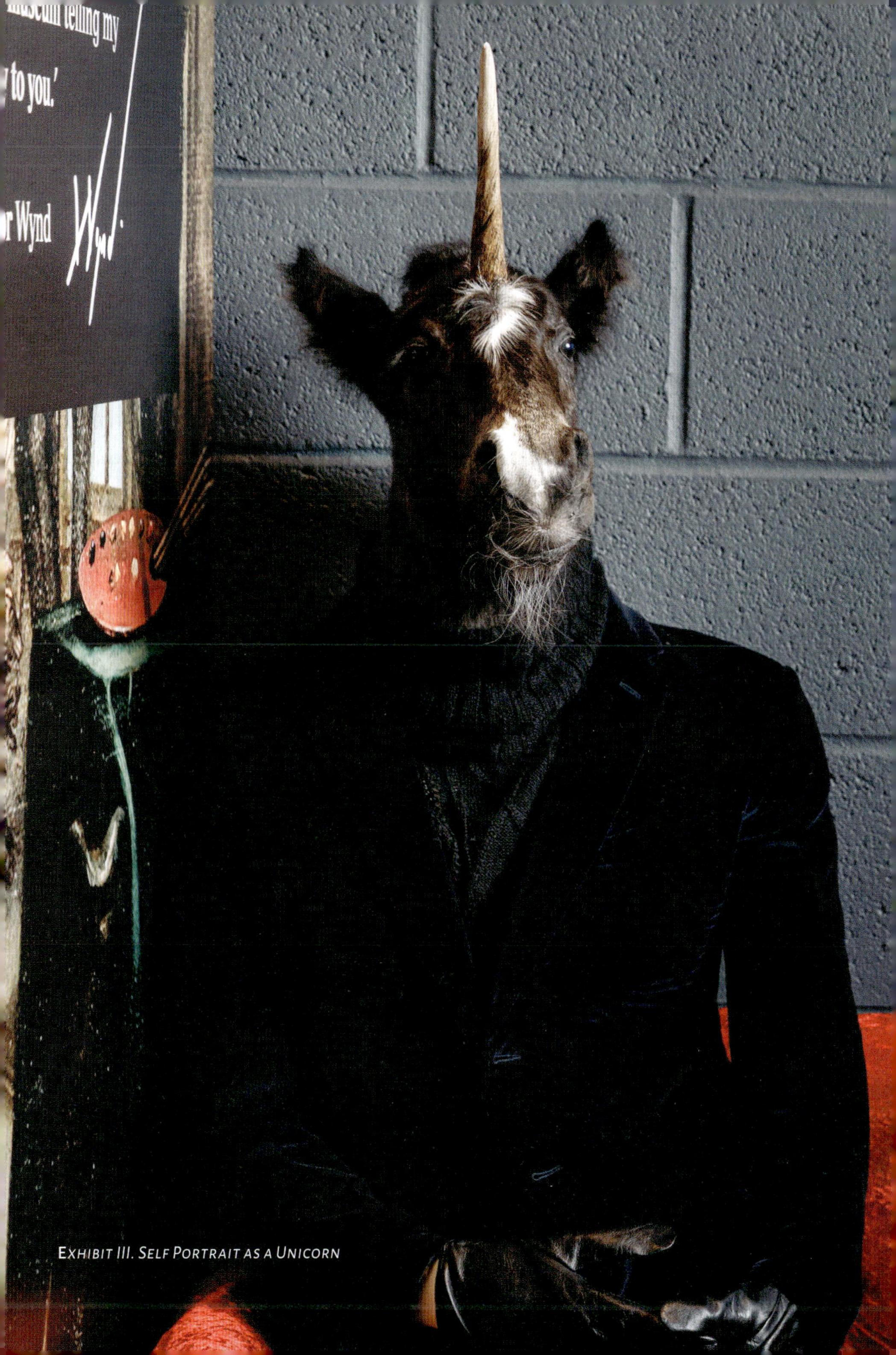

EXHIBIT III. SELF PORTRAIT AS A UNICORN

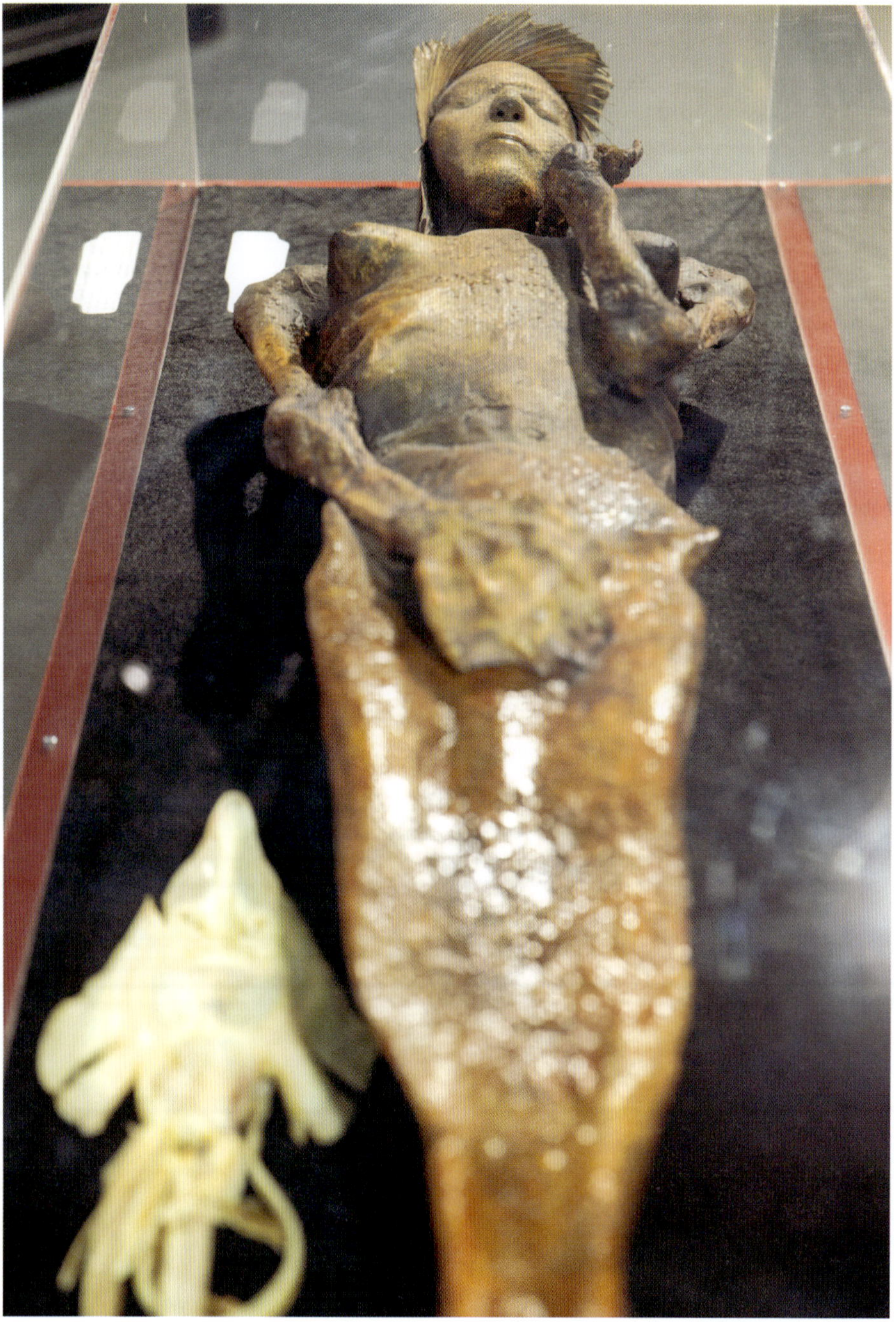

Exhibit IV. Mummified Mermaid in perspex Sarcophagus and preserved Basilisk

III. Self Portrait as a Unicorn

I've always fancied myself as a goat, a sort of deformed Leprechaun. At more than one of my parties I've even dressed up as one and had a lot of fun. So I set about casting my own body and creating a mannequin of myself, but with a taxidermied goats head, ibex horbs and cows feet and legs beneath the shins. Once made I put him in my clothes and expected to have a good laugh, but strangely something else happened, I felt an odd attraction to this creature, I enjoyed getting him dressed and undressed, trying on different clothes. I found myself moving the creature to the breakfast table and talking to it, a lot. One evening, feeling particularly lonely and miserable I dressed it in my silk pajamas and took him to bed. I found he was soft and cuddly and that I slept better than I'd slept for weeks. Since then I've been making a few more, a family of Self-Portraits, a family of friends, including this unicorn that has, until very recently, been sharing my bed, I'm planning to do a pig next.

IV. Mummified Mermaid

I bought this mermaid in a junk shop in Plymouth in the late 1980s. I had never seen anything like it and even though I had just started collecting dead people and felt that I should try and concentrate on one thing at a time she sang to me and I felt that a mermaid could slip through. Such creatures were brought back fairly regularly in the early days of exploration and, when in the hands of a real showman, like America's P.T.Barnum, could make their owners a fortune as all and sundry would line up to see a 'real mermaid'.

V. Jar of Moles for Divination

Moles have of course always been used in magic and in folk medicine: their very appearance counts against them, they are the classic denizens of The Other World - dark, hidden and mysterious: They are often used for their power of divination, a mole is believed to be able to burrow deep into a mystery and find out what has happened, so when you need to find out a person's innermost secrets you use a mole. A dead mole must be kept near to the person for at least a week - the longer the better, so they can be hidden underneath someone's bed, in their kitchen, or these days, for a taxi driver, courier or lorry driver underneath their seat. The mole must be recovered, it's belly cut open and entrails examined. Fresh moles can be used but they are not as powerful as preserved ones as they can only stay near the person for a short time before they start to smell and rot, for this reason contemporary service magicians will always have a jar or two of moles preserved in alcohol or formaldehyde.

VI. Scrying Jar of Urine

Urine has since the most ancient of days been used for Scrying, the attempt to see the future more commonly believed to exist in crystal balls. These days a service magician will look into a jar of the client's own urine, but in olden days the urine of powerful magicians was used - there are plenty of accounts from the middle ages, and even into early modern times, of English & Welsh practitioners using a jar of what they claimed to be Merlin's wee. I have had my own fortune told in a little booth on Venice Beach for $50, in a jar of what was claimed to be Edgar Cayce's micturition. This jar I bought, together with the dead moles, from a practicing Service Magician in The West Country in 2012 for £500, unfortunately he was out of sorts on the day I visited so I have never seen it in action.

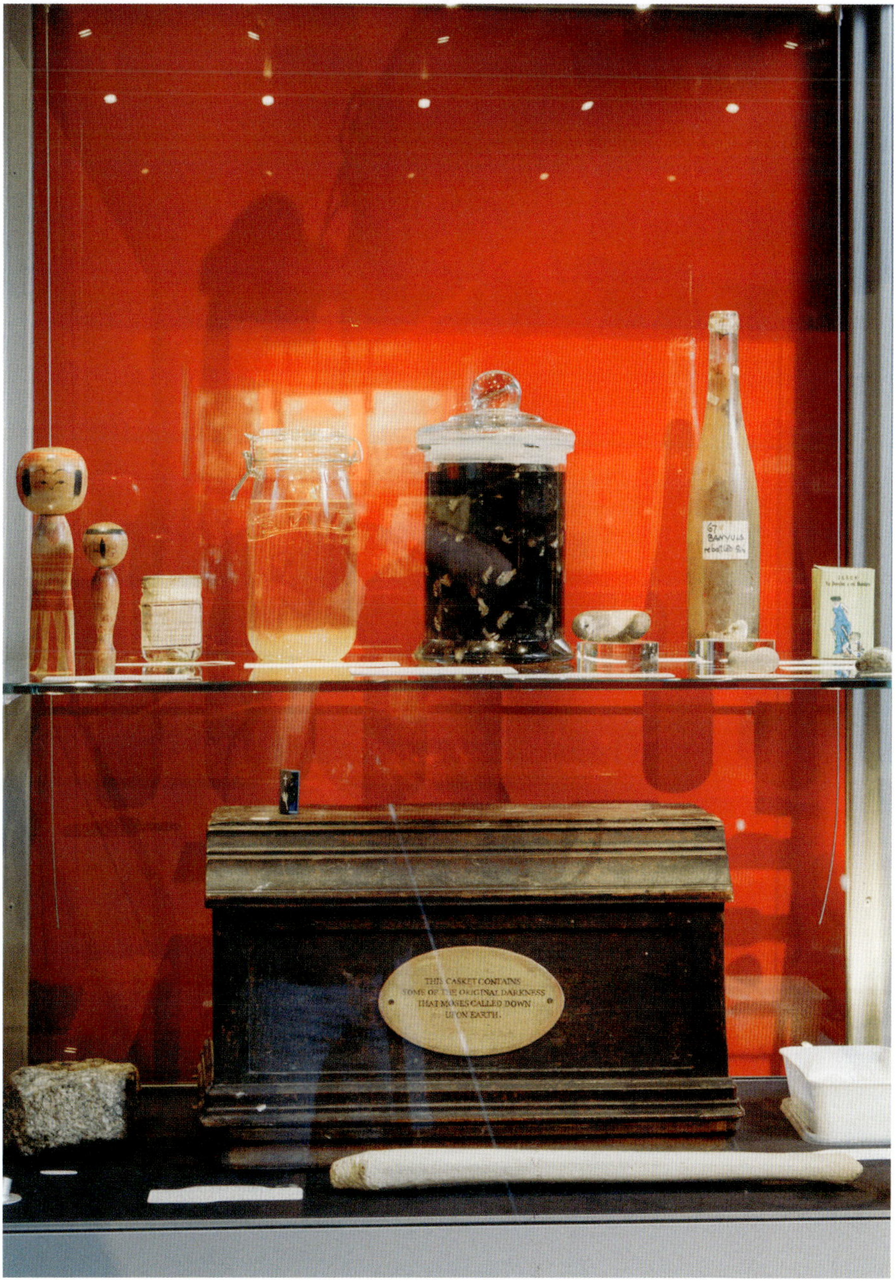

The Cabinet of Magic & Mystery containing, amongst other things, a Jar of Moles used for Divination, Urine for Scrying, Magical Soap & Pebbles & Kokoshi Dolls

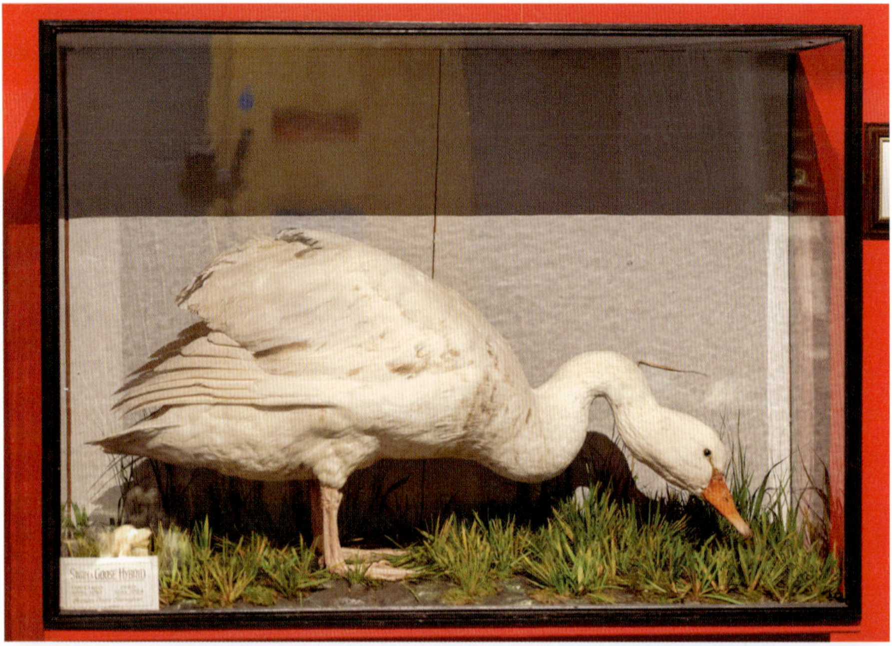

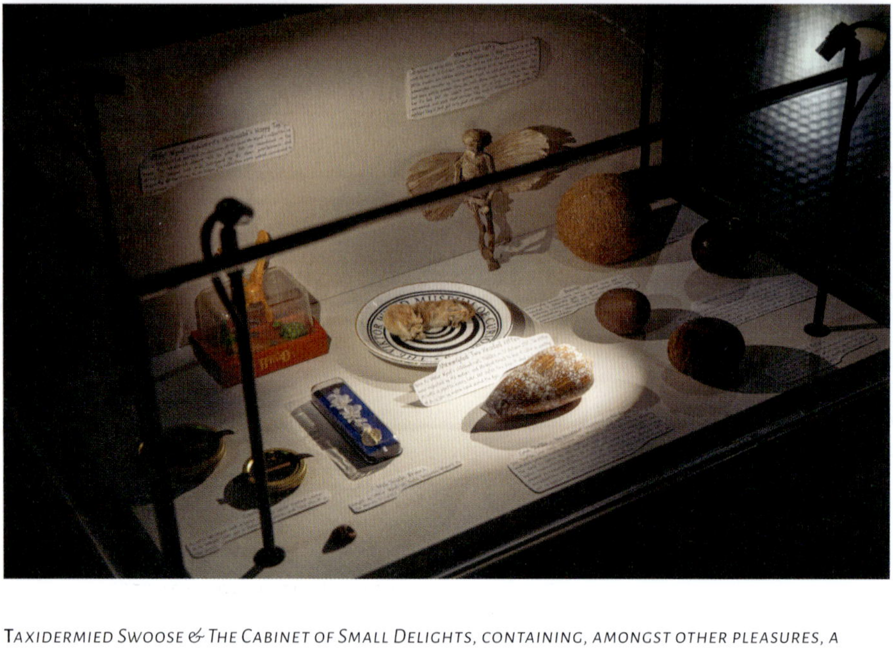

Taxidermied Swoose & The Cabinet of Small Delights, containing, amongst other pleasures, a mummified fairy & two headed kittens, a bezoar, baked potato, fish scale jewelry & Mr.Wynd's sometime favourite McDonald's Happy Meal Toy ...

VII. Giant Seed Pod

I bought this seed pod for £10 from a young boy at Fakenham's Thursday Market in April 2019, he advised me not to plant any of the seeds because, so he told me, if I did whilst they would grow, they would grow very, very tall indeed and if I were to climb them I might have a nasty surprise. So instead I took it home and dried it.

VIII. Bezoar

In olden times Bezoars were more valuable than gold and mounted in elaborate gold and gem studded holders in medieval treasuries. They were believed to possess quite extraordinary supernatural powers including being a universal antidote, potentates fearing death by poisoning from the Shahs of Persia to The Holy Roman Emperors would anxiously dip theirs in their drinks. The Sixteenth Century French Royal Physician Amboise Pare was something of a skeptic who unusually for his day liked to experiment to see what treatments worked and did not work: wishing to test the efficacy of a Bezoar he procured a cook who had been sentenced to death for stealing silver and made him drink a poisoned draught in which Pare dunked a bezoar on the promise of his life if he survived. He spent seven hours in agony before dying, however whilst Pare was convinced others merely muttered that he'd used the wrong type of poison and carried on convinced of the bezoar's power. I am in love with my Bezoars – few things are capable of giving me such intense feelings of pleasure, for me they are more beautiful, and infinitely rarer, than pearls. In fact they are very similar to pearls as they form in the gastrointestinal tracts of mammals, often around alien objects, perhaps a tooth that has either been swallowed or grown in the wrong place: perhaps an ever enlarging ball of hair, this is slowly polished and perfected by the animals gut into the most perfect and most beautiful shiny spheres.

VIIIa. Baked Potato

On the 4th February 2020 Mr.Wynd put this potato in the aga for his lunch.. The next morning, as he put his sausages in the aga he discovered it. Thinking it rather beautiful he has kept it and displays it here for you to admire.

VIIIb. Orange Peel

Whilst driving these exhibits down to Cornwall for you to see Mr.Wynd pulled over on a layby on the A12 and managed to peel this orange in one piece. A great personal triumph.

IIIc. Trobriand Island Cricket Ball

When the Trobriand Islands, in The Soloman Sea, first came to the attention of The West following the publication of Malinowski's The Sexual Life of Savages in 1929 they became as much fabled as The Islands of Love, where sex was merely a fun activity enjoyed by all without hang ups, as a place of nasty wars & anthropophagi. In an effort to distract the locals minds from sex and fighting optimistic missionaries introduced cricket, however it swiftly took on a life of its own with enormous teams of over 50 and games that went on for up to a year, with the scoring of points being the excuse for much celebration and even libidinous dancing, fighting and general mischief. Collected by Viktor Wynd October 2019

XI. Nose Stone

Nose Stones are known to have been used against evil since ancient times. John Stearne (c.1610-1670) - an associate of the terrifying Witchfinder General Mathew Hopkins - was reported to hold one in his hand and put it on the table in front of suspected witches. If it twitched he knew the woman was a witch. This stone was found with a small cache of other magical objects and a mummified cat in a bricked up cavity of Blyford Hall, a Tudor House, in Suffolk.

XII. Heart Stone

This heart stone was found on Suffolk's Shingle Street Beach on the 13th February 1988 by Viktor Wynd and given to his love the next day. It was an unlucky stone, he was told that flowers were preferable and she didn't accept the stone or invitation to dinner.

XIII. Nipple Stone

Historically Nipple stones were used by Cunning Folk and Wise Women to encourage the flow of milk in cows and humans. Rotating one around a nipple, or an udder, 12 times clockwise was supposed to help with the flow of milk. But if you rotated one thirteen times anticlockwise the milk would dry up. These days they are mainly used for pleasure.

XIIIa. Hag or Adder Stone

Since the earliest of times pebbles with natural holes in them have been believed to have the power to deter evil and been left around the entrances to houses and livestock barns. The holes were believed to be formed by the dripping venom of hibernating adders.

XIV. Magical Soap

Mr.Wynd bought this soap on 5.1.2012 in the Witches Market in Mexico City - home to the disciples of Santa Sangre - Holy Death, the patron saint of Drug Dealers, Murderers and all those who feel themselves beyond the reach of a compassionate church, where men with rippling muscles, adorned with heavy gold chains could be seen buying baby goats. Amongst the strange herbs, potions and living owls there was a stall selling magical soap for all occasions, from a student's success at exams, the accumulation of wealth or even to make men fall at the feet of beautiful women and worship them (titled 'I dominate my Man').

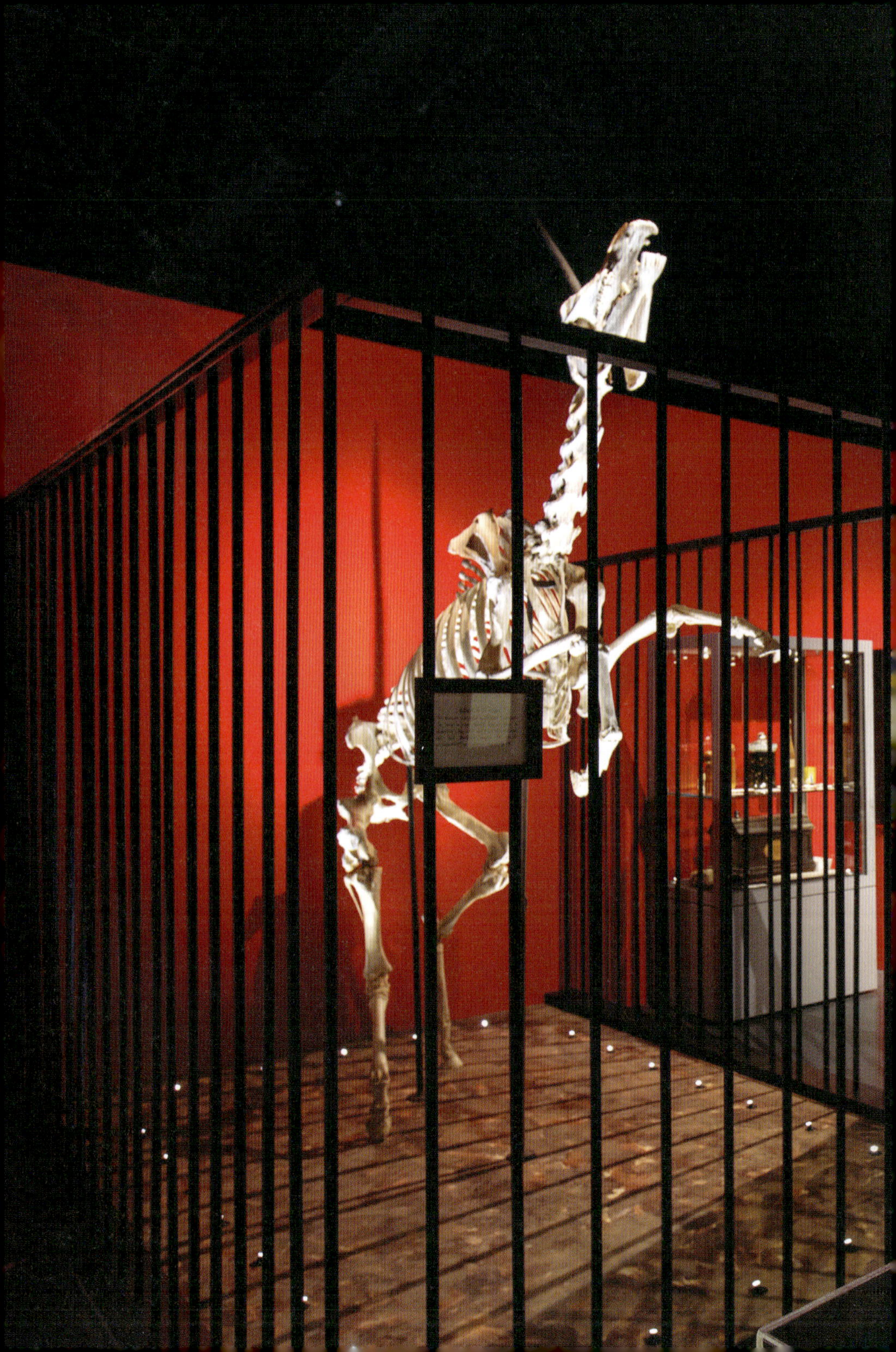

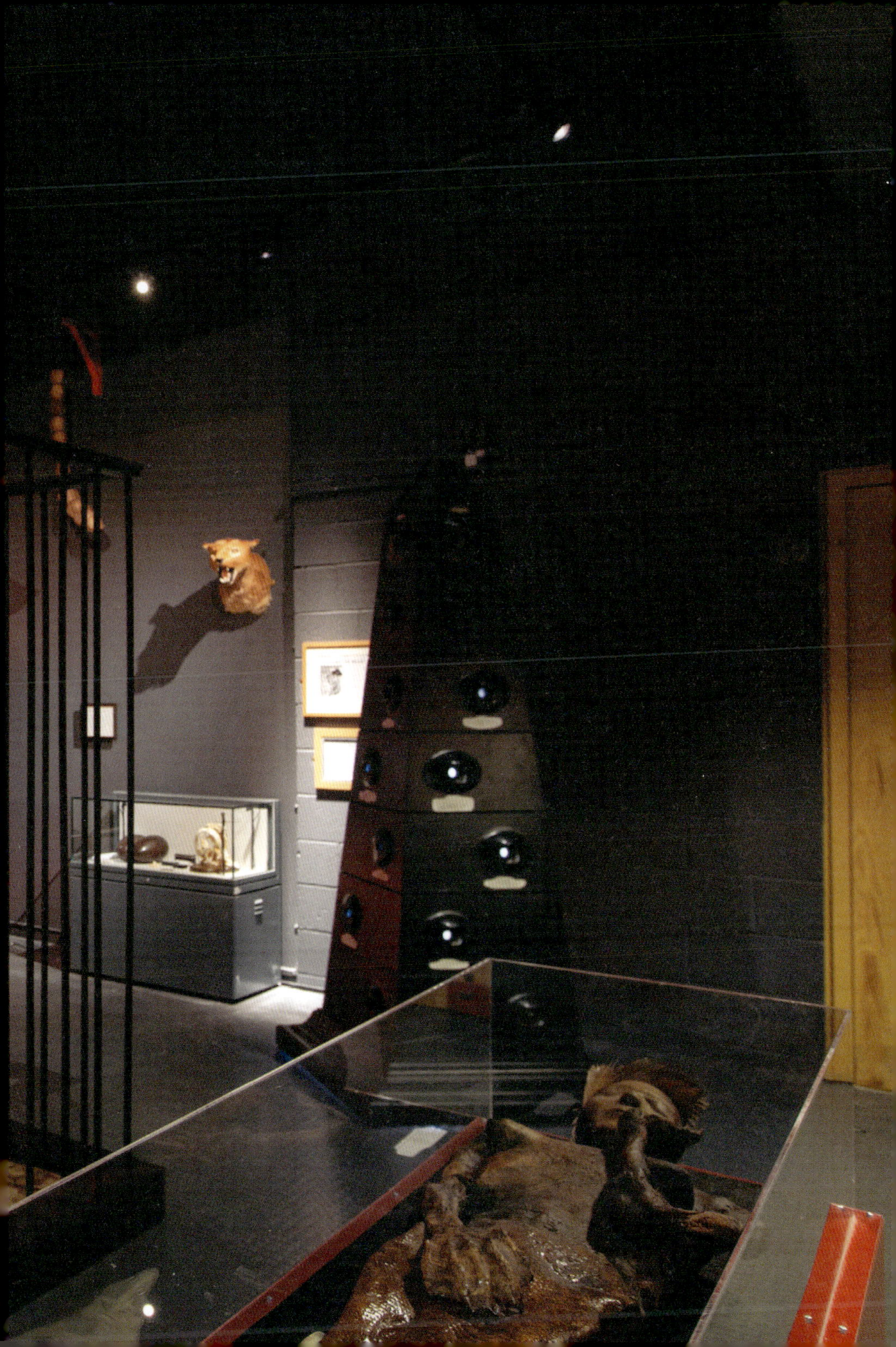

XV. Kokeshi Dolls

In Japan I always try and find a few of these wooden dolls to add to my collection. In the Edo period (1603-1868) they seem to have served as spirit vessels - given to children on their birth to guard and look after them: once the child came of age his child soul would enter the doll that would then be ritually burnt so that the smoke could carry the soul back to it's native mountain but when a child died prematurely its soul and memories could be kept alive by placing the doll on the family altar. Recently my children have taken to stealing them from my study and playing with them and I'm not sure how appropriate this is.

XVa The Elephant in The Room

A magnificent taxidermy specimen of an adult African Bull Elephant, prepared by Rowland Ward for Prince Phillipe of Orleans in 1897

XVI. Coco de Mer

The seed pod of a mysterious deep sea plant that sometimes washes ashore on the beaches of The Indian Ocean. Long valued, perhaps to the excess of the original, for it's resemblance to human bottoms.

XVII. Osik - Walrus Penis Bone

Most mammals, and indeed all primates save humans possess penis bones or bacculum, this has led many in the Biblical community to believe that the rib that God made Eve out of was in fact a mistranslated penis bone, with the perineal raphe the scar. These bones used to power the hydraulics of male reproductive organs come in all shapes and forms. The Walrus's is by far the biggest, known to the Inuit as an Osik, sometimes beautifully carved, they were much used as weapons. A tiny percentage of the male population is still born with a residual penis bone.

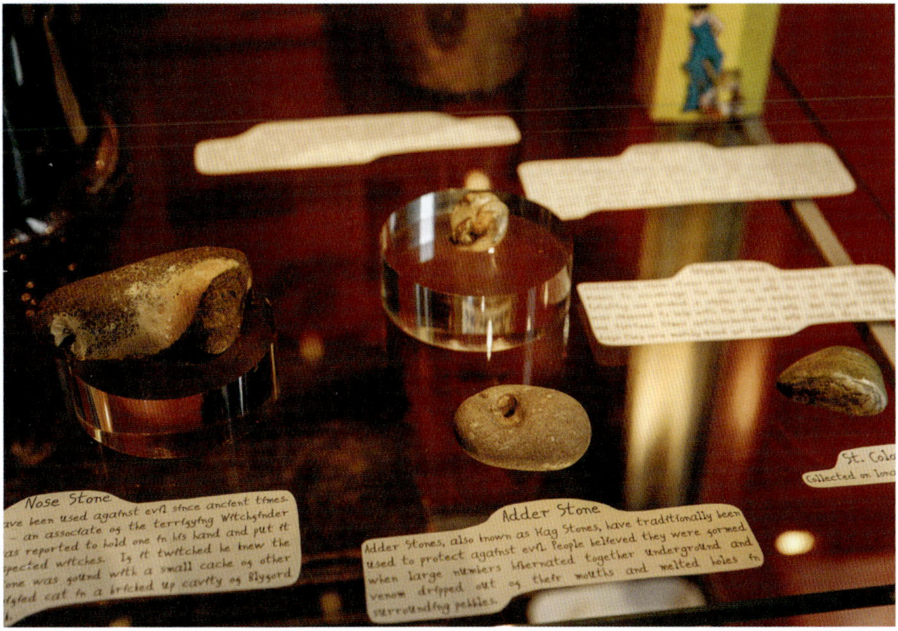

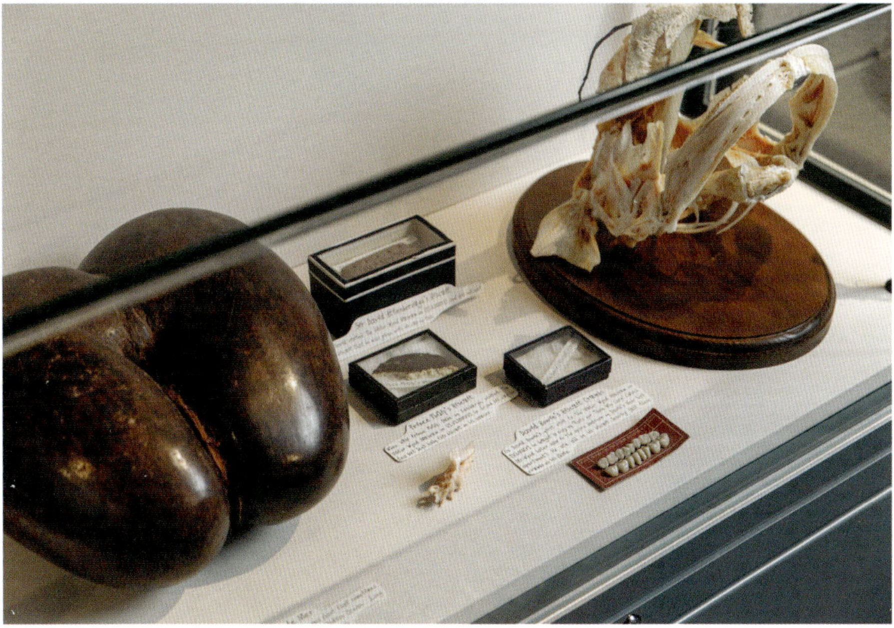

Nose & Adder Stone from the Cabinet of Mystery. Coco de Mer, Wels Catfish Skull & Biscuits bitten, nibbled on and neglected by David Bowie, Prince Philip & David Attenborough in The Biscuit Cabinet

XVIII. Cone Shells

These shells are not only beautiful but also deadly, indeed they are the deadliest creatures on the planet. These snails live off fish which they hunt, kill and eat, being slow themselves they can not outrun prey instead they must lay in wait and when a fish is close enough dart the fish and inject it with a deadly cocktail of hundreds of different alkaloids, enough to kill the fish almost instantly so it doesn't have a chance to swim of and die and be eaten by someone else before the shell catches up with it. The Textile Cone Shell releases 'The Nirvana Cabal' into the water- a modified form of insulin that causes a passing fish to fall asleep allowing the shell to catch up, kill and eat said fish. Several people have died after inadvertently picking up a shell and being stabbed, today a huge amount of research is being made into their poisonous alkaloids with a non addictive painkiller more powerful that morphine being developed, but not so popular as it's not addictive or so profitable.

XIX. Radioactive Sea Shells From Fukishima

Donated to The Viktor Wynd Museum (& museum's across the world) by The International Atomic Energy authority in 2018 to serve as a warning against the terrible dangers of radiation. The common scallop has been genetically altered so that it forms bubbles in it's shell whist the other shell spirals anti clockwise. This was perhaps the saddest mollusk in the sea - all shells spiral clockwise, except this one, whose reproductive organs will also have been in the wrong place and therefore unable to mate, without it finds another anticlockwise shell.

XX. Wels Catfish Skull

This skull is from a Wels catfish that was caught in the Lea Valley, on the edges of London. The Wels catfish is the largest freshwater fish in Europe and a great terror, given their vast size and ferocious appetites it is of no surprise that they frequently occur in myths and legends. In Japan under the name of Nomazu they are believed to live deep in the mud below the country and to cause earthquakes with their wild wigglings when their jailor, the God Kashima lets his guard down.

My favourite story is told by The Nestor Chronicler in his Povist' vremennykh lit (Tale of Bygone Years, circa 1111) of a pre-Christian community by the Slavutych River (the modern day Dnieper in Ukraine) who were ruled for generations by animist Shaman's, who, as they lived by the will of the river that provided their food and transport links, but also threatened them by flooding and other extreme events, managed to somehow convince themselves that the Slavutych was governed by some sort of malevolent Deity who took on the form of an enormous fish and needed to be placated by regular feeding with any old scraps with a special feed, maybe of a piglet or a fowl as Spring came to an end to allow the summer to be released with its bountiful harvests. After a series of disastrous harvests and endless winters (which might coincide with the mid sixth century climate disaster when Byzantine historian Procopius recorded of 536, in his report on the wars with the Vandals, "during this year a most dread portent took place. For the sun gave forth its light without brightness ... and it seemed exceedingly like the sun in eclipse, for the beams it shed were not clear," which modern climatologists think might have been caused by a volcanic eruption), a priest or elder or shaman decided that the water spirit was not happy and needed a proper sacrifice, in short it needed a human baby, and from then on at the end of every spring a new born baby would be fed to the enormous fish, and perhaps because this seemed to placate the monster - the catastrophe was not repeated, crops flourished, and new born babies were every year fed to the fish (or river spirit), until a wandering Knight did battle with the monster, killing it with his lance and converting the community to Christianity, and perhaps giving rise to the legend of St.George.

XXI. Mummified Fairy

Entrusted to me by Alice O'Connor in Aughleam, Co Mayo, Ireland on my last visit to her (of several pilgrimages he made to hear her tales) on 12 October 1999. She sent me into the attic to bring down a little wooden box hidden behind the chimney. In it, she explained, were the mummified remains of three fairies that she had found as a child. They had been fairly common then, she said, many people saw them if they knew how to look and were receptive, but she hadn't seen any for a long long time, no, not, she said since the first motor car came to Mullet in the 1920s and people had started to speak English. No, she said, since The English had begun to be spoken on The Mullet the Good People had left, apparently one word of the English was enough to make them run - even the Catholic Priests in the old days had chased them off by reading the Bible in English to them, she said. Then she murmured and said that perhaps they hadn't disappeared, altogether - perhaps they'd just got very good at hiding.

XXII. Mummified Two Headed Kitten

Born to Viktor Wynd's childhood cat, Tiddles, on 31st October 1969. The kitten was rejected by it's mother and Mr.Wynd tried to keep it alive by feeding it with a pipette every hour, but after two days it died so he mummified it in a jar of warm sand behind the aga.

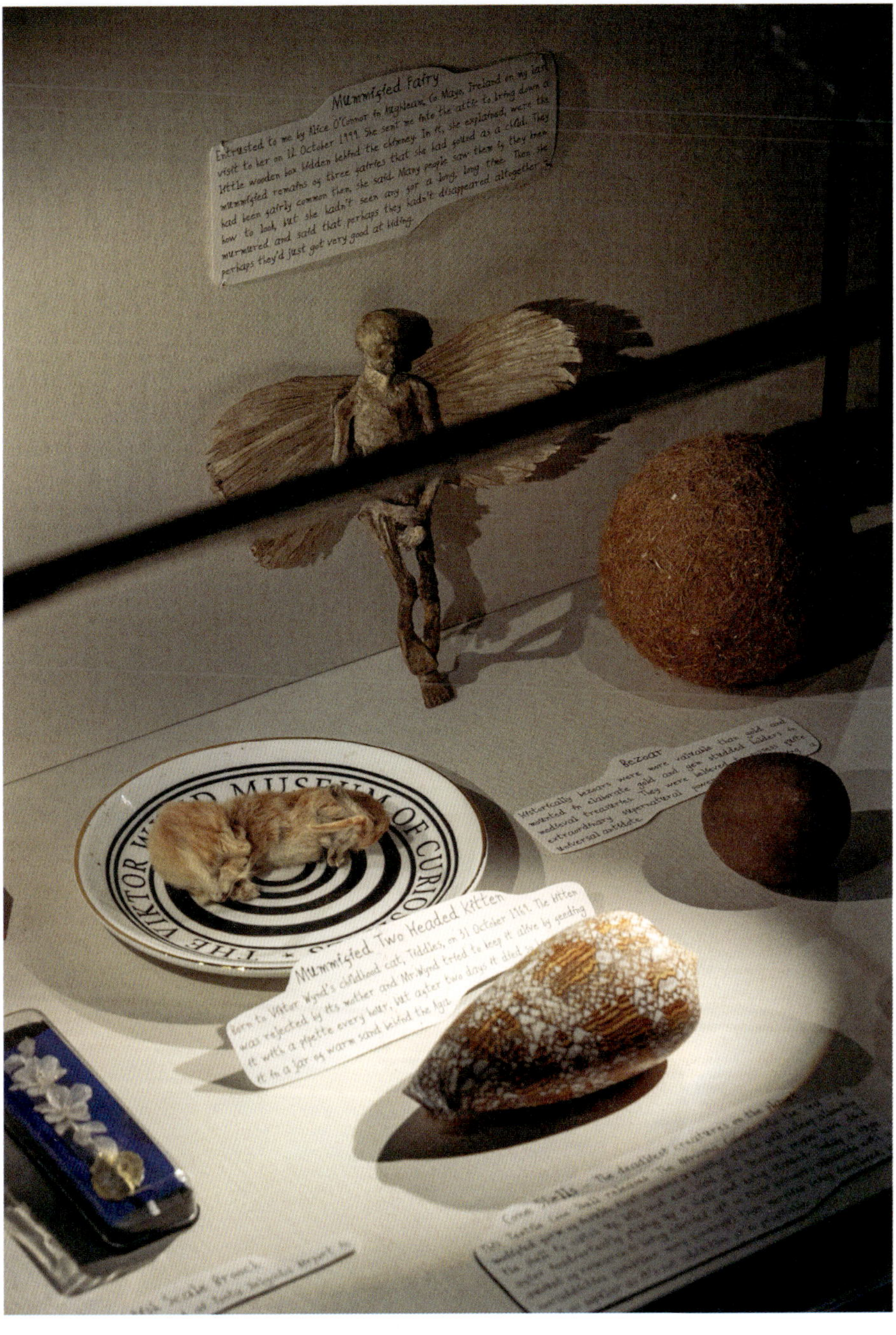

THE CABINET OF SMALL DELIGHTS WITH EXHIBITS (CLOCKWISE FROM LEFT XXI, XXII, XVIII & VIII)

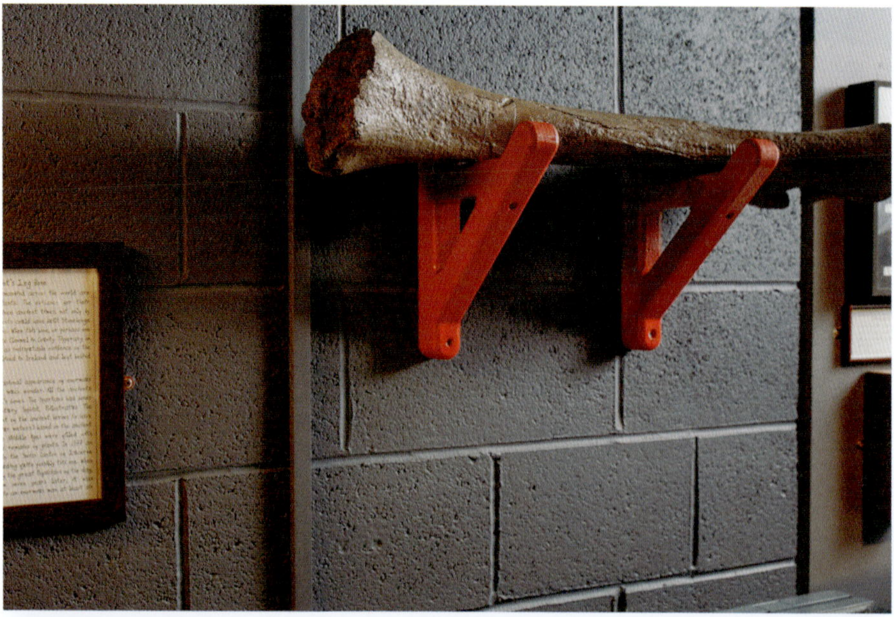

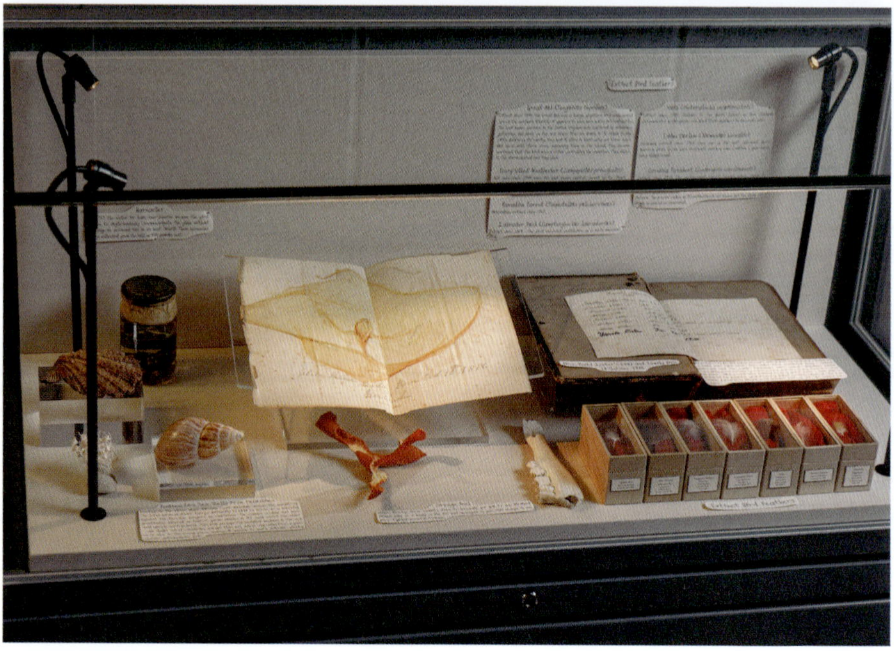

Exhibit XXIV – an Irish Giant's Leg Bone (top) & The Cabinet of Extinct Birds & Radioactive Seashells – With Alice Maud Lister's Caul – October 18th 1876

XXIII. A Basilisk

Pliny tells us that the Basilisk could kill just by breathing or even looking at you and by the Thirteenth Century they had become an even more terrible creature of myth or legend - hatched by a toad from a spherical shell less egg laid by a seven year old cock bird during the days of Sirius the Dog Star, virtually impossible to kill except with a weasel or just possibly a mirror... Basilisks have been staples of Cabinets of Curiosities since they began to be catalogued: everyone had one from John Tradescant to Don Sattero, taking in Emperors and fairground fraudsters. I wanted one and tried to find one and couldn't so I decided to try and make one and went to Billingsgate fish market and bought a thornback ray which I took back to Suffolk, cut about and popped in the Aga's bottom oven over night, where it burnt, looked a bit like my baked potato, and filled the house with a horrible fish smell. The next one I hung in my greenhouse, it made the place smell pretty foul, but it did attract more flies for my tree frogs and insectivorous plants. Once dried I have to say I was rather pleased with it - the flesh had dried back to reveal a protruding arch of cartilage resembling folded arms, the nostrils had become great eyes, with rather charming eyelashes fashioned out of the olfactory laminae.

XXIV. An Irish Giant's Leg Bone

The myths and legends of human kind across the world are littered with stories of Giants, the evidence for whose existence has been obvious to all since ancient times, not only by their works - who else but Giants could have built Stonehenge - but by their physical remains. When this bone, or perhaps one like it, was unearthed outside Clonmel in County Tipperary on the 4th January 1621 it was seen as indisputable evidence of the Great Giants that had once lived in Ireland and left behind so many great monuments.

XXV. Alice Maud Lister's Caul & Family Bible October 18th 1876

Less than 1 in 80, 000 babies is born with a piece of membrane - known as a caul, over their head. Such babies were considered lucky - indeed powerful, and the caul's themselves much valued - midwives would carefully preserve them by removing them, then drying them on, a piece of paper. Such a relic was itself believed to be of great power - and able to preserve the possessor from drowning. Bought by Viktor Wynd at The Low House, Laxfield in Suffolk on 10th December 2019 for £85 but valued much higher.

XXVII. Extinct Bird Feathers

- Passenger Pigeon (Ectopistes migratorius)

Extinct since 1 September 1914. A migratory North American bird whose vast numbers darkened the skies. They were considered a sacred bird by the Wyandot people (or Huron), who believed that every 12 years, during the feast of the dead, the souls of their dead would migrate into the passenger pigeons and be eaten. But, with the arrival of Europeans who liked to eat them, kill them as pests and destroy their habitat, their days were numbered.

- Carolina Parakeet (Conuropsis carolinensis)

Extinct since 1918. The northernmost parrot species, whose range is supposed to have reached up the east coast of North America as far as Ontario. The precise cause of its extinction is not known, but the blame can firmly be placed on man.

- Ivory-billed Woodpecker (Campephilus principalis)

Not seen since 1944 when its last known habitat, owned by the Singer Sewing Company, was logged in northeastern Louisiana.

- Great Auk (Penguinus impennis)

Extinct since 1844, the great auk was a large, flightless bird widespread across the northern Atlantic: it appears to have been eaten into extinction. The last known specimen in the United Kingdom was captured by some fishermen gathering sea birds on the sea stack Stac an Armin in St Kilda in the 1840s. Aware of its rarity, they kept it alive in their bothy for three days. But as a wild storm arose, marooning them on the island, they became convinced that the bird was a witch controlling the weather. They killed it, the storm abated and they fled.

- Labrador Duck (Camptoryhnchus labradorius)

Extinct since 1878 – the first recorded annihilation of a North American bird.

- Eskimo Curlew (Numenius borealis)

Presumed extinct since 1963. Once one of the most numerous North American birds, with some 2 million a year being slaughtered in the late 19th century.

- Huia (Heteralocha acutirostris)

Extinct since 1907. Endemic to the North Island of New Zealand. Exterminated by Europeans, who used their feathers to decorate hats.

- Paradise Parrot (Psephotellus pulcherrimus):

Australian: extinct since 1927.

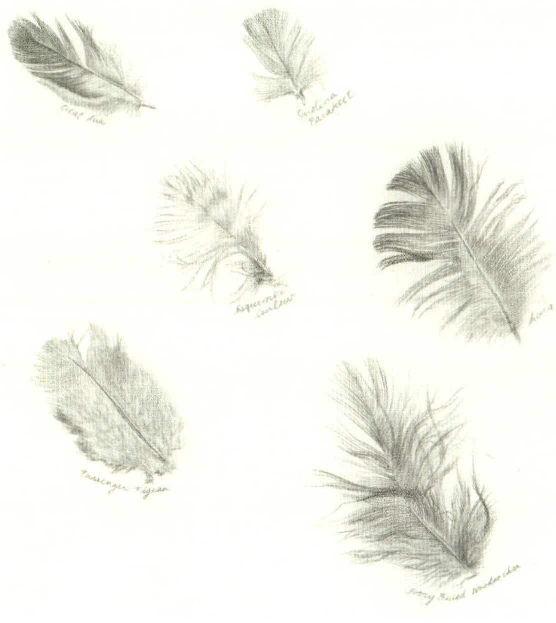

EXHIBIT XXVII. EXTINCT BIRD FEATHERS, DRAWING BY CATHERINE WALLIS

XXVIII. Entomological Specimens

Collected by Viktor Wynd on his extensive travels until in 2016 he decided that killing insects just for the pleasure of pinning and framing them was wrong

XXVIII. Sir David Attenborough's Biscuit

Sir David visited The Viktor Wynd Museum on III.X.MMXII and did not eat this biscuit that he was given with his cup of tea.

XXIX. David Bowie's Biscuit Crumbs

On David Bowie's first visit to The Viktor Wynd Museum on IV.I.MMXI he bought a copy of 'Rats for Those Who Care' CWhich Mr.Wynd later saw in the spare bedroom of David's New York apartment. He ate the whole of his biscuit leaving just these crumbs on his plate.

XXIXa. Prince Philip's Biscuit

When HRH Prince Philip, Duke of Edinburgh, visited The Viktor Wynd Museum on VI.VI.MMXVI He drank his cup of tea but left half this biscuit on his saucer.

XXX. Casket

A casket containing some of the original darkness that moses called down upon earth.

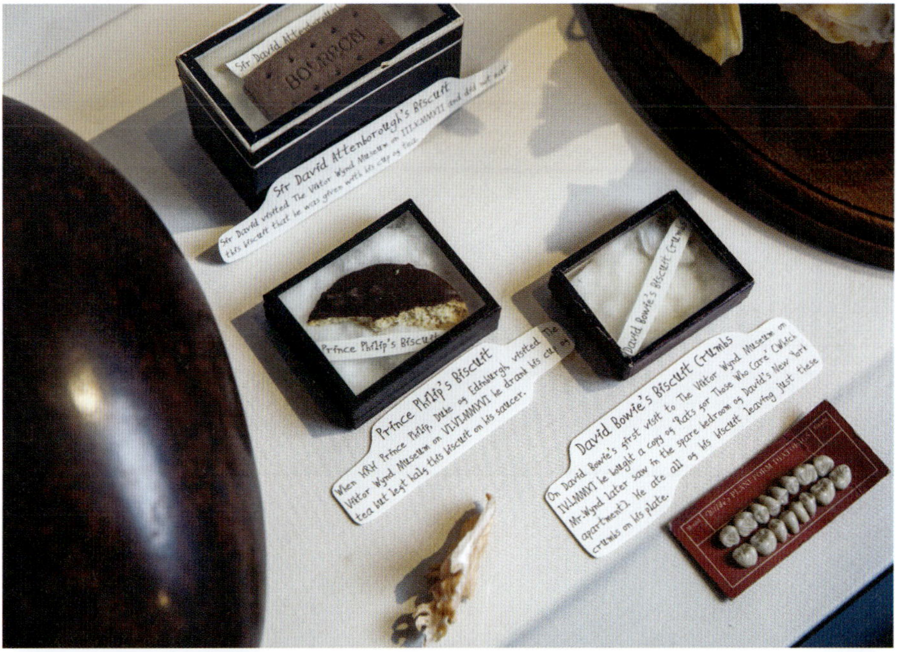

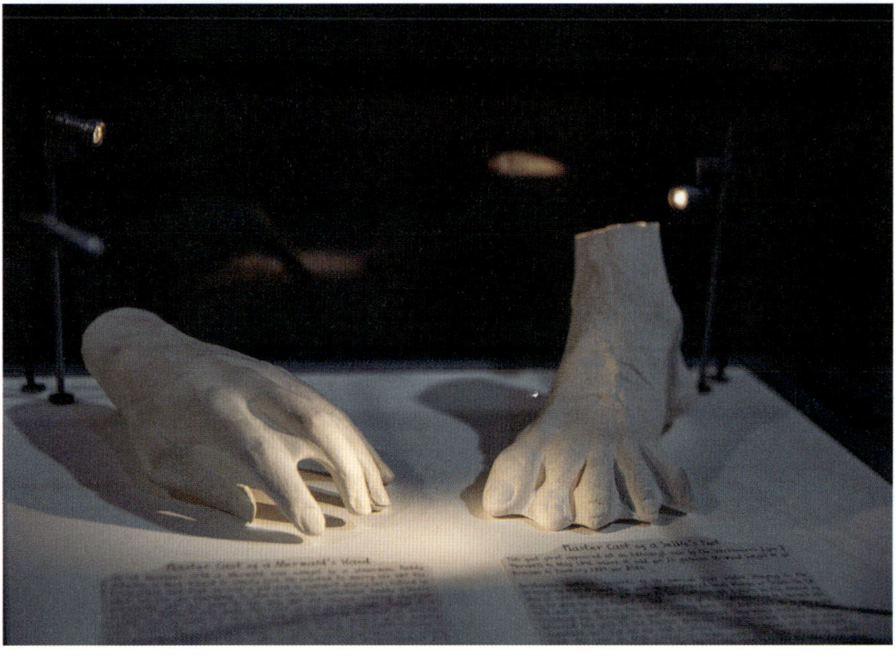

Celebrity Biscuits in The Biscuit Cabinet & Plaster Casts of a Mermaid & Selkie's hand and foot

XXXI. Plaster Cast of a Mermaid's Hand

On 16th December 1798 a Mermaid was caught by fisherman Paddy O'Dwire on Bere Island in County Cork. He wanted to marry her but the local priest said that she was a fish and he couldn't marry her, indeed he must let her go. Unwilling to live in sin the reluctant Paddy O'Dwire eventually put her back in the sea, but not before visiting physician Dr.Stephen Maturin had made this cast of one of her hands. Though it is possible that he made the story up and this is the merely the cast of someone with syndadactly - a hereditary condition where humans grow webbing between some digits on their hands or feet, especially as the hand appears to be male and there are no records of the mermaid outside of Dr.Maturin's notes. It is worth bearing in mind that Bere Island is even today a remote place and there is no reason to suppose that anyone would have written down this story there even were it to be true, perhaps all that can be said is that it is an 18th century cast. Purchased by Viktor Wynd at Sheppard's Auction Rooms, County Laois in October 1995 for £250.

XXXIa. Plaster Cast of a Selkies Foot

Dr.Stephen Maturin records in his journal that whilst staying in The Orkneys he took this cast from the foot of a captured Seal Woman or Selkie. On the 18th March 1802 Mrs.Flett got back to her cottage at Lyness on the island of Hoy to find her son Robert in bed with a girl. On questioning it turned out he'd met this girl on the beach, pulling back the bedcovers in a fury she examined the stranger's feet and discovered they were webbed. She then marched the girl to the Factor, Malcolm Stuart's house, where he cross examined her and as she had no story tended to agree with Mrs.Flett's that she was a seal woman or Selkie and had been planning, after seducing Robert Flett, to take him to the sea and drown him. Dr.Maturin examined the woman and noted that she was about forty years of age and took this plaster cast of one of her webbed feet. His journal, now in the archive of the Royal Naval College, does not record what happened to the woman. This cast first appeared at an Edinburgh sale by the auctioneers Lyon & Tunbull in May 1842 where it sold for twenty five guineas. Mr.Wynd bought it at Bonhams in January 2009 for £500.

XXXII. Patrick O'Brian's Banyuls Bottle

The author Patrick O'Brian lived at Collioure in The South of France for almost 50 years, he had a small vineyard and made his own wine. This bottle was removed from his cellar after his death in 2000 and drunk and discovered to be prodigiously good.

XXXIV. Sting Ray Tail

Taken by Mr.Wynd in May 2002 to one of Torture Garden's Infamous Fetish parties in London, and used as a whip, by a friend, in the dungeon.

Identified Deep Sea Worm

In 2005 Viktor Wynd was going through one his periodic bouts of melancholia and found himself repeatedly, endlessly, obsessively drawing worms. It seemed to make him feel a little better. He found, and bought, this worm at a Shell Show in Theydon Bois, and it gave him then, and continues to give him now an inordinate amount of pleasure.

XXXV. 10,000 Year Old Deep Sea Sponge

Mr.Wynd bought this at a Shell Show because he thought it was very pretty. When he got it home and looked it up he was horrified to discover that it was the single giant basal spicule from Monorhapsis chuni, an enormous deep sea sponge and at least 10,000 years old. He has sworn not to buy any more but still thinks this one immensely pretty.

XXXVa Stuffed Head of a Big Cat

Run over by Rosemary Roads of Tenstone Farm, Bodmin on the 7th January 1988 and given to local amateur taxidermist Joan Goodenough who mounted the head and presented it to Jamaica Inn, from where it was purchased by Viktor Wynd at the famous auction in 2003.

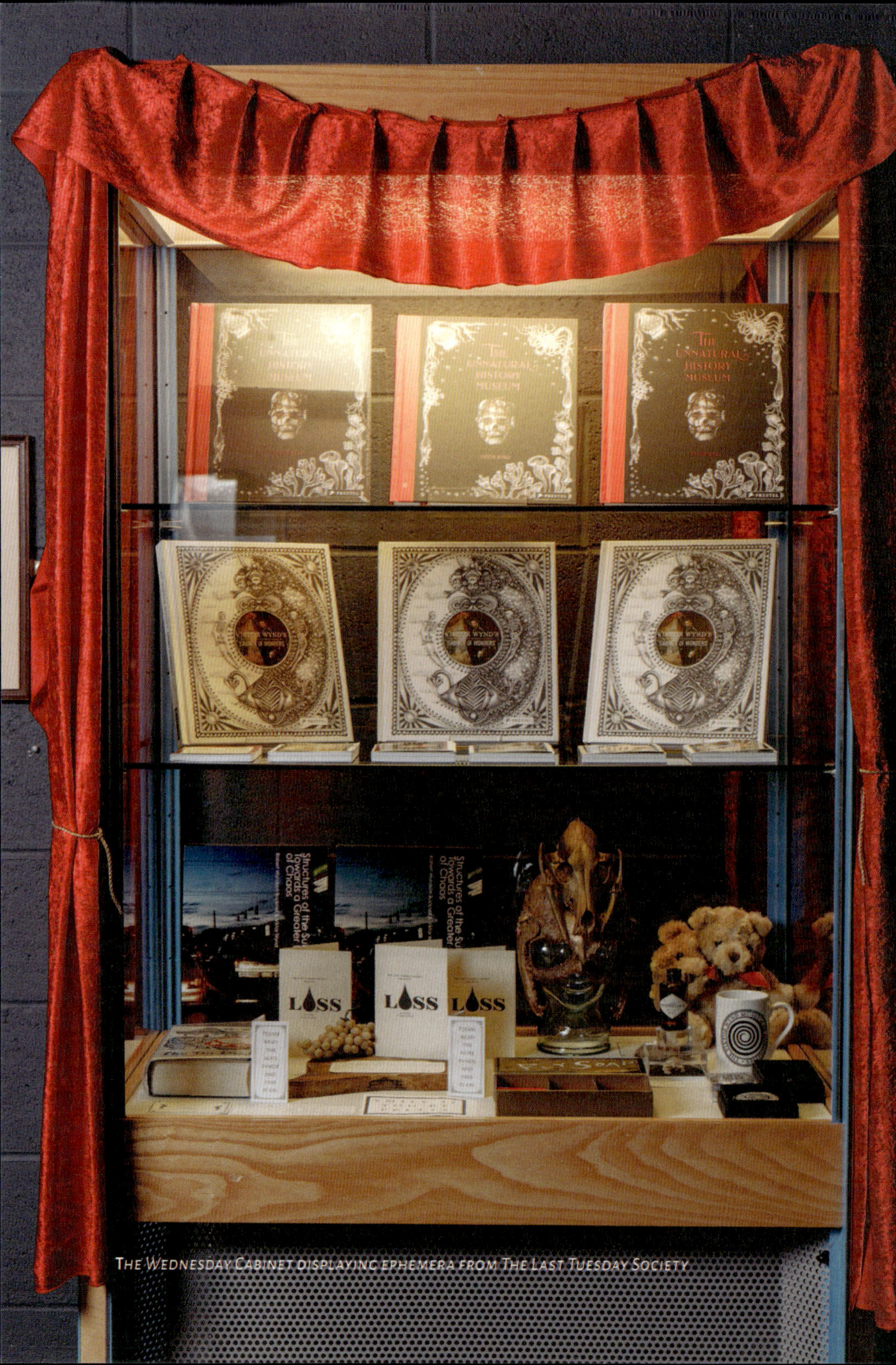

THE WEDNESDAY CABINET DISPLAYING EPHEMERA FROM THE LAST TUESDAY SOCIETY

The Last Tuesday Society Ephemera

The Last Tuesday Society is a 'pataphysical organisation founded by William James at Harvard in the 1870s. Viktor Wynd was inaugurated as it's Chancellor in the early noughties, and since then has put on a bewildering wall of events, exhibitions, installations and other wonders, including, but not limited to, Magnificent Balls, Seances, a Literary Salon, Magic Lantern Shows, a Festival (Wyndstock), art Exhibitions, a curiosity shop, expeditions to Papua New Guinea & The Congo.

XXXVI. Chopping Board & Invitation from Loss an Evening of Exquisite Misery

In 2006 Viktor Wynd reinterpreted Gunter Grass's Onion Cellar night club from The Tin Drum. The basement of Mayfair Nightclub 43 South Molton Street was transformed with dead flowers & animals, broken children's toys and crushed red velvet. The saddest musicians and artists performed, a very sad man with a smile box went around giving people £1 if they smiled and £2 if they laughed, guests came in their hundreds, dressed in decaying beauty, and at midnight Mr. Wynd gave a rousing speech '101 Reasons to Cry Today' and then handed out chopping boards, knives and onions - and everyone chopped onions and cried. It was great fun.

XXXVII. Viktor Wynd's Mask

For Ten years Viktor Wynd put on ever more dazzling and spectacular Masquerade Balls for up to 5000 guests with many hundreds of performers - from a 100 piece classical orchestra playing waltzes to a snake wrangler, naked boys and ladies painted gold would drop oysters into guests mouths. Unfortunately Mr. Wynd can remember very little of this decade but this is one of the Masks he made.

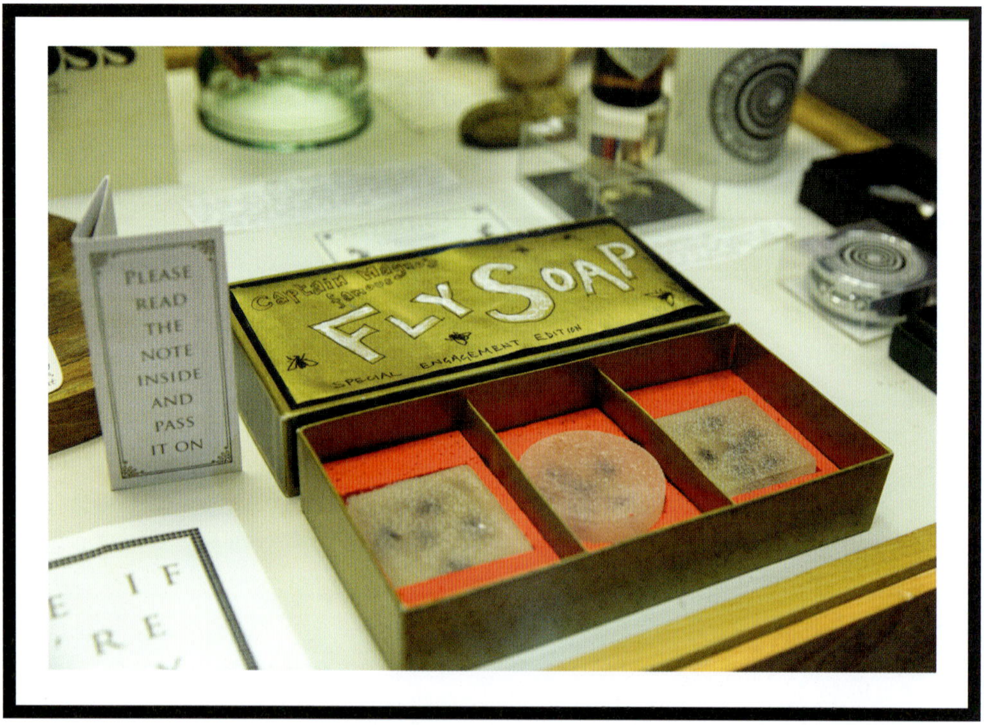

XXXVIII. Viktor Wynd's Favourite McDonald's Happy Toy

This is the Toy that sparked an obsession. At it's peak Mr.Wynd's collection of Happy Toys numbered almost 400, he found this one abandoned on the street in Miami and as intrigued by it's sheer pointlessness and stupidity. All the items in his happy toy collection were found abandoned in the street.

XXXI. Fly Soap

A kind and generous engagement present to Mr.& Mrs Wynd from the artist Magnus Irvin (perhaps best known for his chocolate anuses).

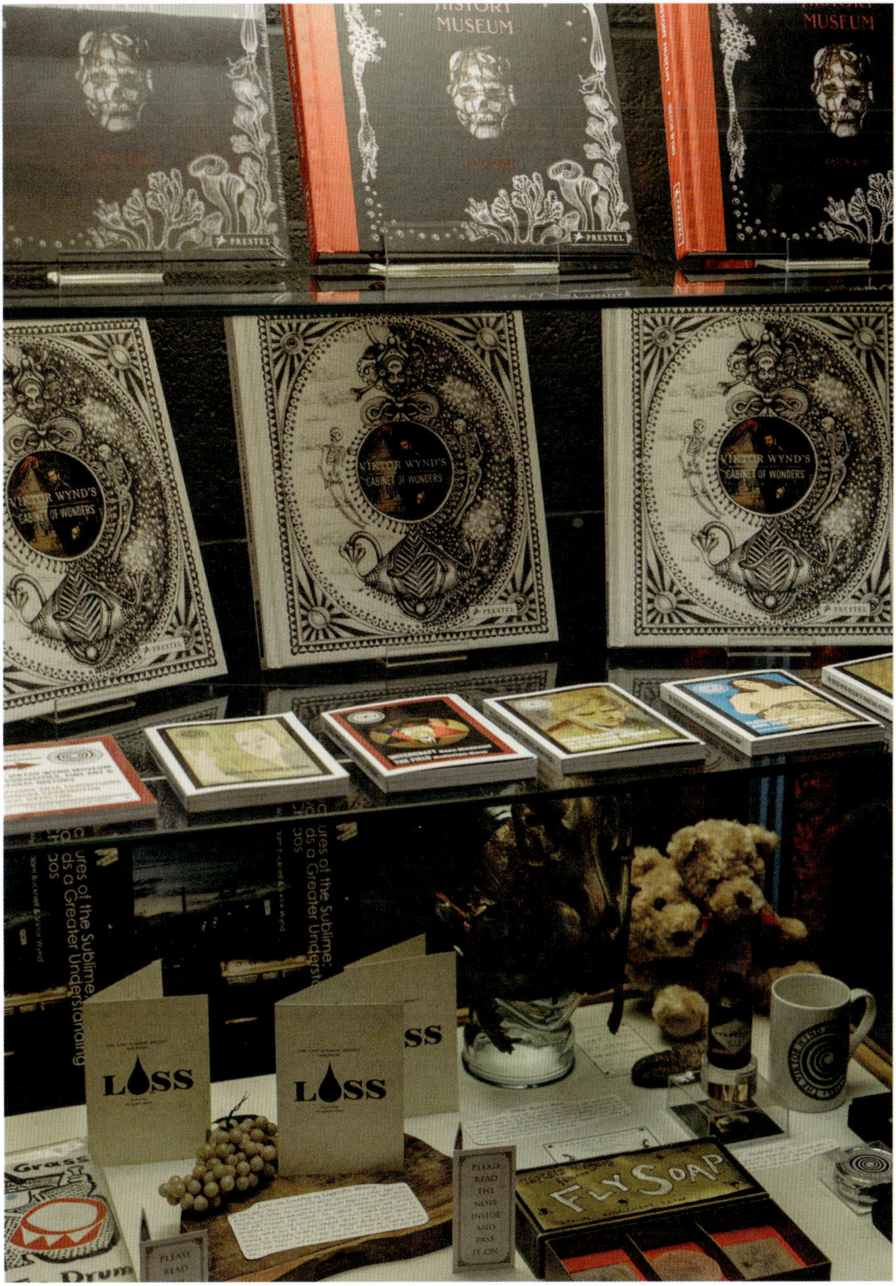

Books, Exhibition Catalogs, Chopping Boards & Invitations to 'Loss; an Evening of Exquisite Misery,' A Two Headed Teddy Bear & Fly Soap in The Wednesday Cabinet

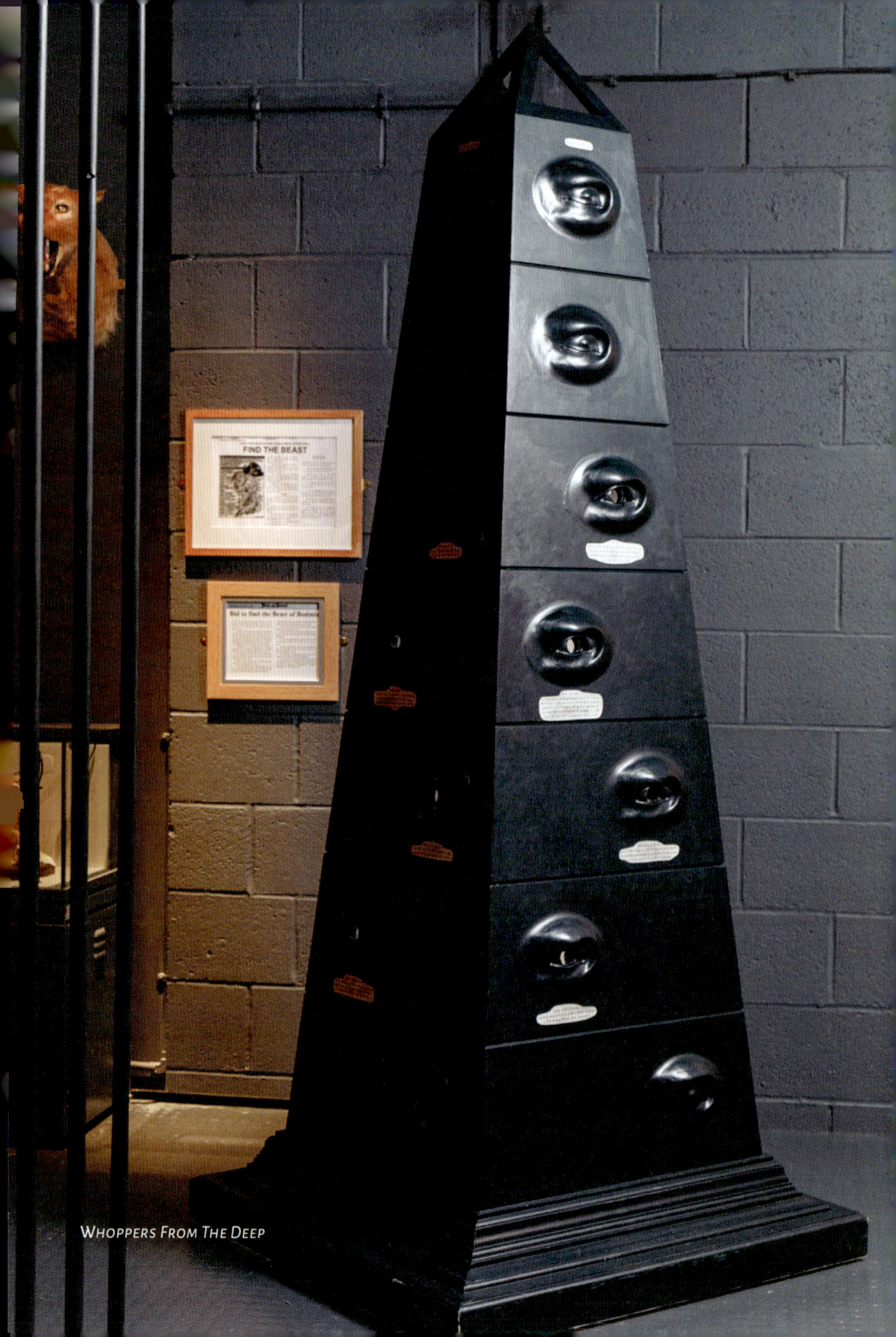

WHOPPERS FROM THE DEEP

WHOPPERS FROM THE DEEP

AN OBELISK, STUDDED WITH CASTS OF A WHALE'S EYE WHERE VISITORS CAN LOOK IN, THROUGH THE EYE, TO A TINY ILLUMINATED DISPLAY COMPARTMENT CONTAINING CURIOUS, LABELLED, ITEMS FROM VIKTOR WYND'S HOME.

Deep Sea Balls

These mysterious, and very beautiful, deep sea balls were found on the beach at Noto, Sicily, by Viktor Wynd on December 20th 2013. Why was the beach wet? Because the Sea Weeda.

Porcelain Dolls Head

19th Century French. Why won't oysters share? - because they're shellfish.

Goose, Rabbit & Fox Poo

Collected, and plasticated, by Viktor Wynd in September 2018. Who keeps the sea cleaned - mermaids.

Porcelain Suffolk Spirit Creatures

Made by Viktor Wynd Septmeber 2019. Why does the ocean roar? You would too if you had crabs on your bottom.

Tin Toy

Given to Viktor Wynd as a child, never played with and recently found in a suitcase underneath Mr.Wynd's childhood bed at his parent's house.
How do you make an octopus laugh? Ten Tickles.

Canary Island Pine Cone - Pinus Canariensis

Collected by Viktor Wynd at the Caldera de Taburiente, La Palma, Canary Islands January 2018. Why won't sharks eat clowns? Because they taste funny.

Cricket's Birthday Party

Given to Mr.Wynd by his brother Michael who thoughtfully bought it for him in Beijing in 2016. Why are there fish at the bottom of the sea? Because they dropped out of school.

Norwegian Troll

Why are seagulls so luck in love? Because one good tern always deserves another.

McDonald's Happy Toys

From Viktor Wynd's collection of almost 200, found abandoned. What do you call as fish with no eye? A fsh.

Silver Sea Snail

Borrowed from a nautical themed party at The Savoy by Viktor Wynd in 2002 and never returned. What's a pirates favourite letter? (Everyone will say 'Rrrr' and then you say 'you'd think it would be R but it's actually the C. But don't take away their P because then they'd be irate.

Banksia Seed Pond

Banksia grandis seed pod picked by Viktor Wynd in Perth 2nd October 2002.What do you call a man with a seagull on his head?

Cliff.

Emu Egg

Laid by Viktor Wynd's pet Emu, Doris, (who had been known as Boris before laying the egg) in 2016, blown (and made into a delicious omlette). What lies at the bottom of the ocean and twitches?

A nervous wreck.

Pomacea paludosa

Collected by Viktor Wynd 1.3.2002 from Limkin snail pile, Loxahatchee River bank, nr route 706 bridge, Jupiter, Florida.Why did the crab blush? Because he saw Queen Mary's bottom.

Admiral Lord Nelsom

Given to Viktor Wynd as a 30th Birthday present by J.Davies, Esq. and much appreciated.

I once dreamt I'd own an ocean of orange soda but it was just a

Fanta Sea.

Crescent Stone

Found on Falmouth Beach 8.2.2020 by Viktor Wynd. In the Islamic world such stones are seen as powerful protectors against evil. What did one flat-fish parasite say to the other at the end of their date?...

"Your plaice or mine?"

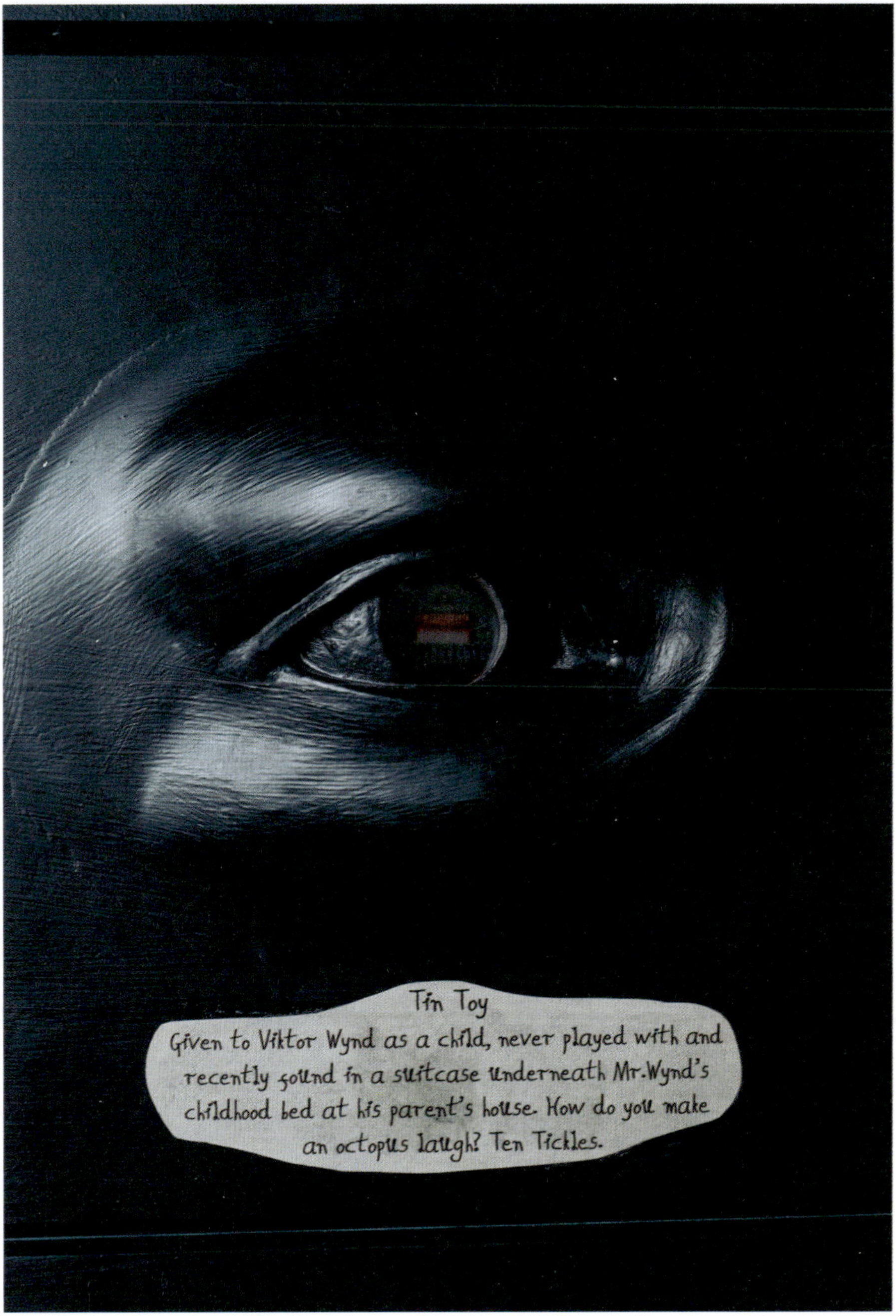

WHOPPERS FROM THE DEEP - TIN TOY

STORY TIME WITH VIKTOR WYND

VIDEO PIECE MADE IN COLLABORATION WITH BILL JACKSON

Telling stories is central to Viktor Wynd's practice, for the past twenty five years he has been learning stories by heart, from The Brothers Grimm to The Arabian Nights, reworking and retelling them in performances across the country.

In the projection room a film of the North Sea, from the East Coast, is shown whilst a recording plays of Wynd's reworking of several traditional Irish Fairy Tales - featuring real Fairies, Mermaids, a Changeling Child, The Good People, All Hallows Eve, a talking corpse and the devil himself.

MEMORANDUM ON MUSEUMS OF CURIOSITY AND WONDER

Richard Pell (Director, Center for PostNatural History)

One of the unexpected perks of running a museum, is that you discover fellow travellers with wildly different interests, but the same passion for sharing them. No matter the story, the trick is in the telling. But, beyond the particulars of the specialty, there are the museums that know where they come from. They know the about the deep family tree with all its weird cousins, tawdry affairs, and illegitimate offspring: The carnival barkers, sideshows, dime museums, roadside attractions, tourist traps, peep shows, learned pigs, and mermaids that lurk at the very foundation of the modern museum. Viktor Wynd reunites us with these long lost relatives and helps wash off the shame that evicted them from the official story of The Museum. He reminds us that our separate institutional habits of learning, looking, and listening, once all happily shared the same room. Not long ago, the point of a museum was not simply to leave with a set of facts, but to awaken a yearning for wonder as an end unto itself.

Charles Wilson Peale's American Museum, founded in 1786, was the first public institution in the United States to consider the general public as a valid audience for the cultivation of wonder and curiosity. It brought together fine art and natural history such that the visitor was, "led always from familiar objects toward the unfamiliar... into the mysteries of life". One of Peale's foundational specimens was the first complete skeleton of a mastodon to be exhibited anywhere in the world. The mind-blowing nature of this creature, at the time, cannot be overstated. So little was understood about this pre-historic wonder, that it was exhibited simply as "The Great Incognitum" or The Great Unknown[1]. When was the last time you visited a science museum and were shown something so new and incredible that science was at a loss for words to describe it? And yet, isn't this the experience that we want to have? To arrive at the bleeding edge of what is knowable and gaze over the edge into the unknown and ask a question without feeling dumb.

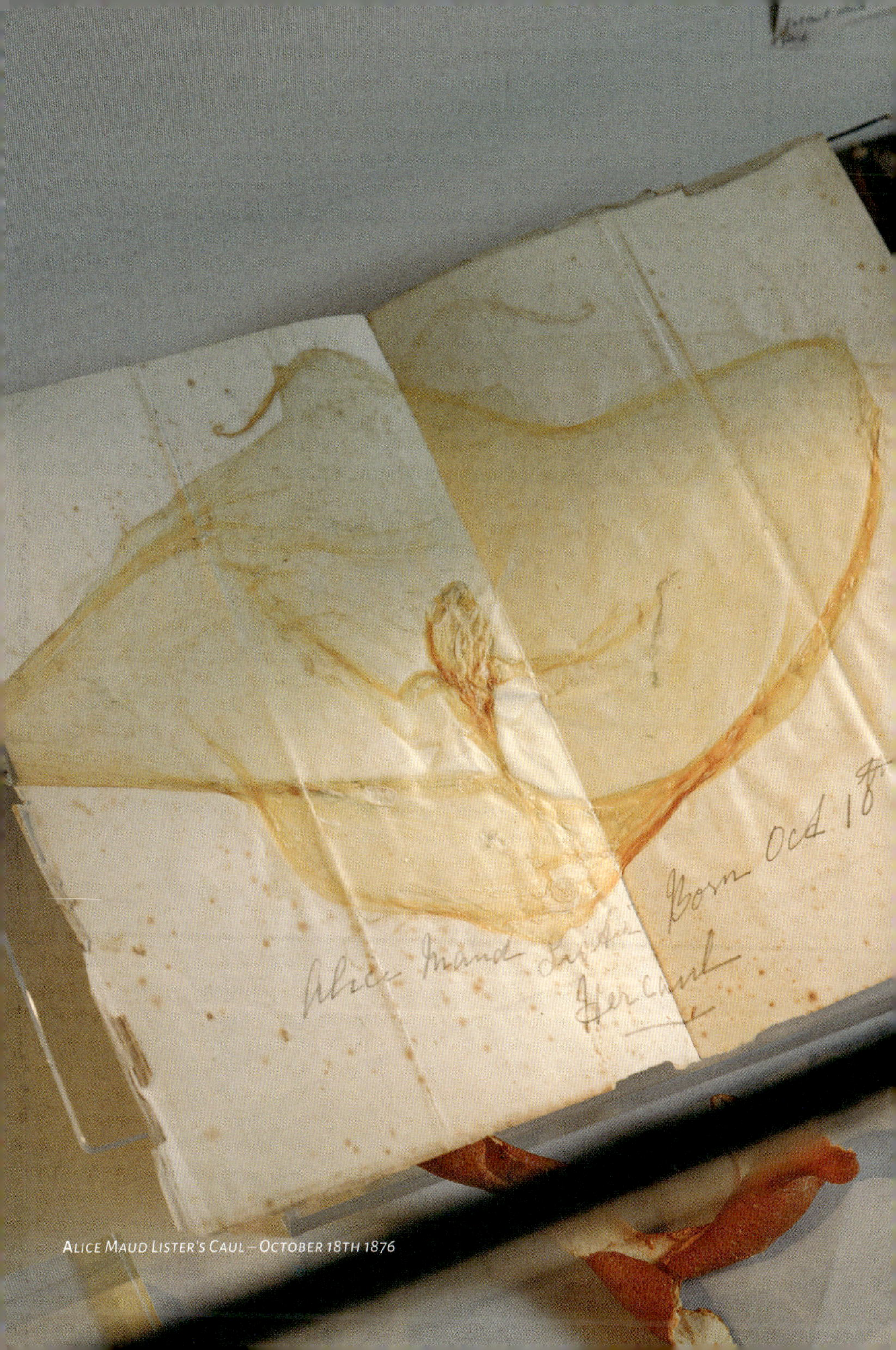

Alice Maud Lister's Caul – October 18th 1876

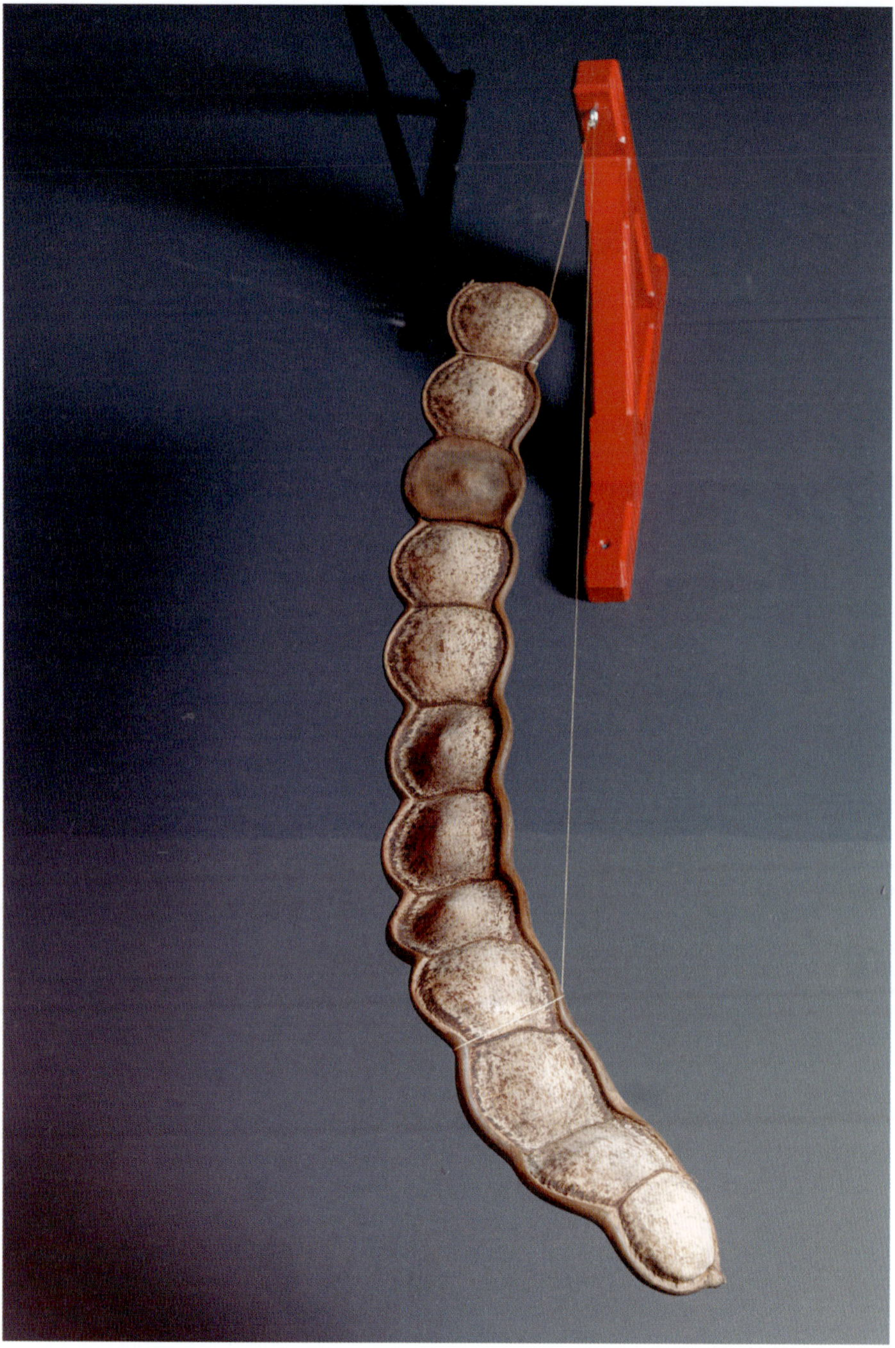

Viktor Wynd's Magical (& Giant) Bean

Most young children freely and unselfconsciously experience wonder. Everything is new and everything is possible. Their curiosity is validated by museums and libraries. For years, in my own museum, I have blurred or ignored the distinction between wonder and curiosity. I often champion them both as a bedrock goal, in contrast to more traditional assessments of knowledge acquisition[2]. However, when I try to split the difference between wonder and curiosity, I realize these are two very different characters. In fact, if "Wonder" and "Curiosity" were people, they would have issues with one another. The two clearly spend a lot of time together, hence the confusion. And they look quite alike on the surface—perhaps they are siblings? If so, I suspect Wonder is the older of the two. Wonder generally describes the emotional experience of encountering something truly unexpected and amazing. Wonder is associated with a child-like way of thinking. Wonder yearns for richly novel experience and when she finds it, doesn't want it to end. Wonder is an ecstatic state of completeness. It requires no further information. There are things Wonder would rather not know. In fact, if Wonder had her way, we probably wouldn't be having this conversation.

The Bible is littered with "wondrous" miracles, from self-igniting shrubbery to extraordinarily efficient lamp oil. The Wonder that they inspire is an entirely appropriate response to the experience of encountering an omniscient God. In this sense, Wonder is a complete experience. The architecture of cathedrals and temples does nothing if not inspire wonder. Its function in part, is to chase away any doubts about who is in charge. It is cathartic, not cerebral. From Day One, the Biblical God advises his two initial followers to steer clear of the fruit of the Tree of Knowledge. And lo, we are all descendants of the pair who first blew off this rule. Children raised in the Christian tradition who ask too many questions are provided with the cautionary, and somewhat gruesome tale of "Doubting Thomas" being commanded to finger his Lord and Saviour's hand-holes in order to prove he's the real deal.

Curiosity, on the other hand, does harbour some doubts. Cautious skepticism may be what separates Curiosity from Wonder. Curiosity always wants to know more and is willing to risk disappointment to achieve this end. While Wonder has its eyes respectfully closed, Curiosity is peeking. Wonder is perfectly happy to visit the Emerald City and behold The Wonderful Wizard of Oz, and stay there forever. While it is Curiosity who pulls back the curtain revealing the truth. Lest anyone forget, the character who exposed the fraudulent Wizard of Oz was neither Dorothy, nor any of her anthropomorphic companions, but rather her tiny dog Toto[3].

Curiosity and Wonder do have something in common: They are both propelled by the unexpected. But, Wonder wants to hold onto the experience, "Please don't ruin it". While, Curiosity takes the risky next step by asking, "Why is it that way?". Curiosity thinks that Wonder is naive. Wonder thinks that Curiosity is a buzzkill. I think they actually need each other. Without an appreciation for

Wonder, Curiosity IS a buzzkill. Left to its own devices, Curiosity would conduct an autopsy on the family cat just to find out how it works (pun intended). And without Curiosity, Wonder would still be staring up at the stars, satisfied that it is the center of the universe. Curiosity hates to admit it, but Wonder tells great stories. Wonder pilots flying reindeer and surreptitiously delivers video games consoles to middle-class kids. But one day, Curiosity kills Santa Claus. It had to happen eventually. Wonder WAS being naive on that point.

At this point, it may sound like I am describing the difference between art and science, or science and religion, or rationality and non-rationality, or left-brain and right-brain, and surely there's plenty of dualisms that rhyme with this idea. But I am mostly describing the inseparability of these things. It is only in the last 150 years or so, that we formally separated these worlds to the point where there are scant few places

that attempt to engage both Wonder and Curiosity on equal footing.

Museums have evolved a great deal in the 180 or so years since their first generation collapsed in financial ruin or adapted into the more lucrative P.T. Barnum-styled collection of freaks, oddities and hoaxes. Following the necessary injection of funds from the mega-wealthy industrialists of the late 19th century, museum collections gained a stunning degree of rational order and quantitative analysis. They subdivided into seemingly unrelated institutions of art, science and history. They also acquired the monumental architecture of cathedrals and temples. The Great Hall in the National Museum of Natural History in Washington D.C. with its colossal taxidermy elephant and adjoining halls of knowledge inspires nothing if not wonder. It is a truly incredible space. But perhaps in the effort to impress the public with how much they know, they created a space that makes it harder to ask "Why?"

I'm not suggesting that the modern science museum is the Great and Powerful Oz, hiding behind his curtain. But I am suggesting that it has erected an edifice of similar proportions. What if, today, the National Museum of Natural History opened a hall dedicated to specimens and artifacts that are not well understood? Call it "The Hall of Incognitums." They might risk visitors wondering about the "wrong things." Visitors might risk being disappointed or frustrated. Competing narratives might develop that call the validity of the whole project of science into question. And meaningful answers to our deepest questions might emerge from unexpected places. It all sounds very risky. Is anyone else curious how it would all play out? I know Mr.Wynd is.

Richard Pell is the founder and director of the Center for PostNatural History, a museum dedicated to the collection and exposition of life-forms that have been intentionally and heritably altered through domestication, selective breeding, tissue culture or genetic engineering. The Center for PostNatural History operates a permanent museum in Pittsburgh, Pennsylvania, and produces traveling exhibitions that have appeared in science and art museums throughout Europe and the United States. Pell is a National Academy of Science KAVLI Fellow and was awarded the 2016 Pittsburgh Artist of the Year. He is an Associate Professor of Art at Carnegie Mellon University.

---

1 *Sellers, Charles Coleman. Mr. Peale's Museum: Charles Willson Peale and the First Popular Museum of Natural Science and Art. New York: Norton, 1980. Print.*

2 *Pell, Richard W. "Can sites cultivate curiosity?" University of Pittsburgh, Pittsburgh. December 10th, 2015. Panel Discussion.*

3 *Baum, L. Frank, and Michael Hague. The Wizard of Oz. New York: Holt, Rinehart and Winston, 1982. Print.*

Hymn to Pan

Thrill with lissome lust of the light,
O man! My man!
Come careering out of the night
Of Pan! Io Pan!
Io Pan! Io Pan! Come over the sea
From Sicily and from Arcady!
Roaming as Bacchus, with fauns and pards
And nymphs and satyrs for thy guards,
On a milk-white ass, come over the sea
To me, to me!
Come with Apollo in bridal dress
(Shepherdess and pythoness)
Come with Artemis, silken shod,
And wash thy white thigh, beautiful god,
In the moon of the woods, on the marble mount,
The dimpled dawn of the amber fount!
Dip the purple of passionate prayer
In the crimson shrine, the scarlet snare,
The soul that startles in eyes of blue
To watch thy wantonness weeping through
The tangled grove, the gnarled bole
Of the living tree that is spirit and soul
And body and brain–come over the sea,
(Io Pan! Io Pan!)
Devil or god, to me, to me,
My man! my man!
Come with trumpets sounding shrill
Over the hill!
Come with drums low muttering
From the spring!
Come with flute and come with pipe!
Am I not ripe?
I, who wait and writhe and wrestle

With air that hath no boughs to nestle
My body, weary of empty clasp,
Strong as a lion and sharp as an asp –
Come, O come!
I am numb
With the lonely lust of devildom.
Thrust the sword through the galling fetter,
All-devourer, all-begetter;
Give me the sign of the Open Eye,
And the token erect of thorny thigh,
And the word of madness and mystery,
O Pan! Io Pan!
Io Pan! Io Pan Pan! Pan Pan! Pan,
I am a man:
Do as thou wilt, as a great god can,
O Pan! Io Pan!
Io Pan! Io Pan Pan! I am awake
In the grip of the snake.
The eagle slashes with beak and claw;
The gods withdraw:
The great beasts come. Io Pan! I am borne
To death on the horn
Of the Unicorn.
I am Pan! Io Pan! Io Pan Pan! Pan!
I am thy mate, I am thy man,
Goat of thy flock, I am gold, I am god,
Flesh to thy bone, flower to thy rod.
With hoofs of steel I race on the rocks
Through solstice stubborn to equinox.
And I rave; and I rape and I rip and I rend
Everlasting, world without end,
Mannikin, maiden, Maenad, man,
In the might of Pan.
Io Pan! Io Pan Pan! Pan! Io Pan!

Aleister Crowley

Notes

Notes

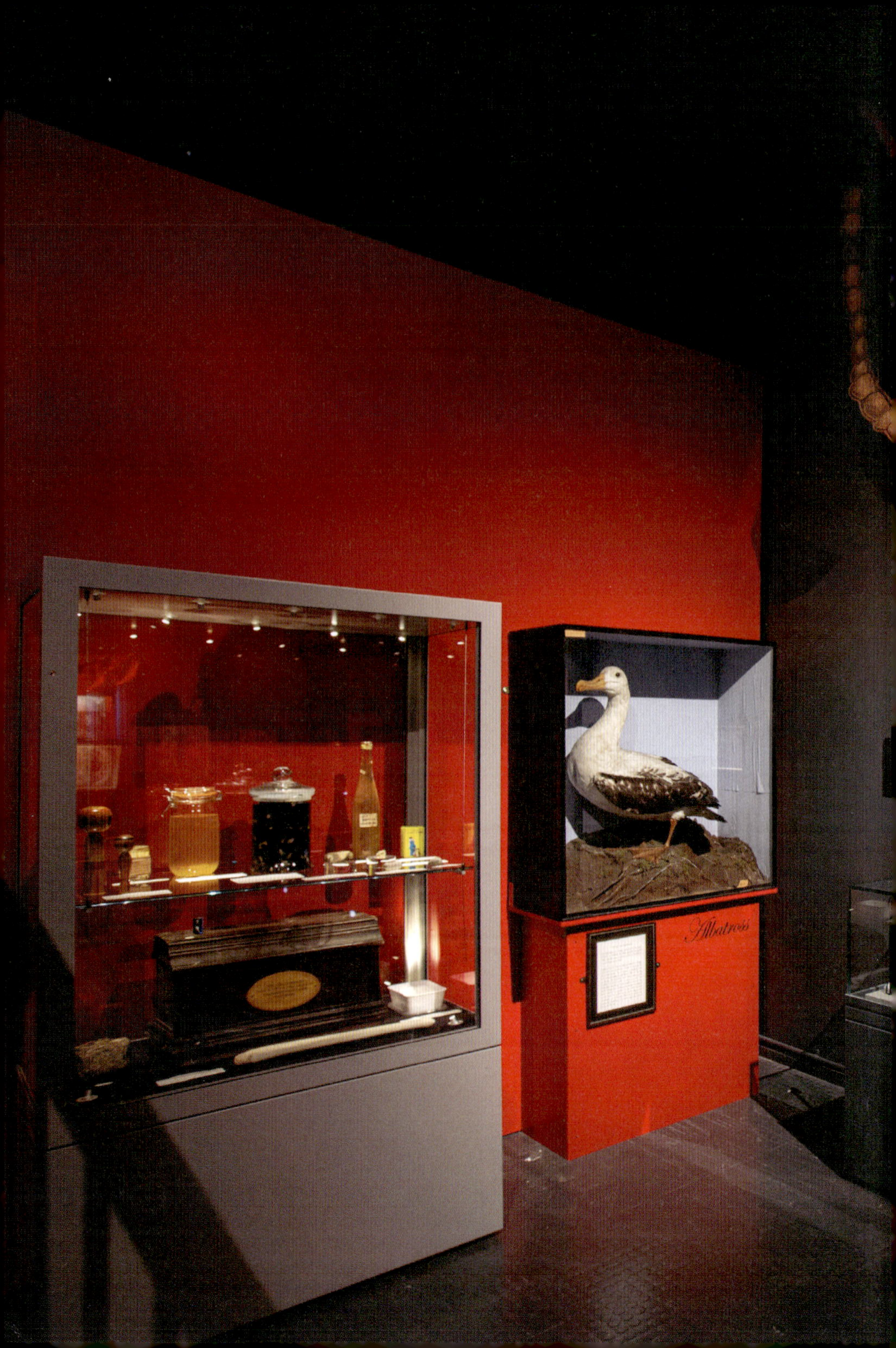
Albatross

Designed by LMNOP Studios
Photos Copyright Kirsten Prisk
Essays Copyright Adrian Dannatt, Mark Dion, Arthur MacGregor
Labels Copyright Viktor Wynd
ISBN Number 978-1-8384596-0-4
Printed by Bell and Bain Ltd, Glasgow

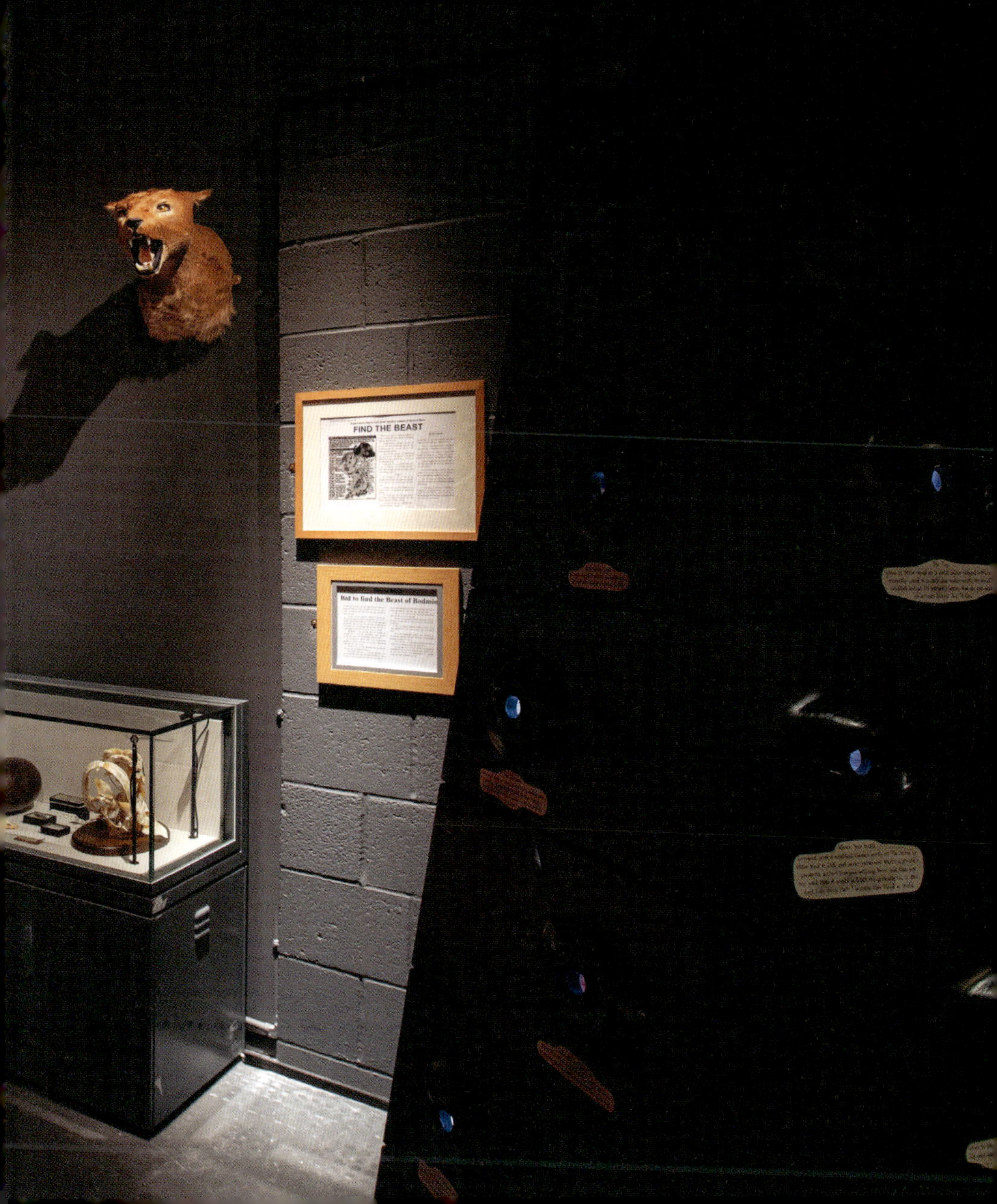